"Oh my life"

Kate Saarinen

ISBN: 978-1-5272-4014-8

Cover design by Spiffing Covers

Published by Socciones Editoria Digitale
www.socciones.co.uk

"After reading Kate's story I vowed never to take good luck for granted again. This book brings into sharp focus what it means to have luck and what it means when luck deserts you.

Put simply, the story is about two people fallling in love and searching near and far for a place to call home. But the devil is in the detail. Luck plays havoc with their hopes and dreams and they find themselves at the mercy of a system stacked against them.

Kate has a knack of making you feel you are right there as things happen, rooting for her and Alex to overcome the latest obstacle in their path. Vividly drawn characters in words and pictures pepper the book and the lively, engaging style of writing will draw you in. I read it in one go - five stars!" **Tuamum**

"This is a great read! A lively tale about finding love, risking everything, being broke and refusing to give up! Kate tells the story with honesty and great humour, with a sobering glimpse of how easily life can go wrong. The book is enhanced by amusing illustrations, mouthwatering recipes and the wit and wisdom of Captain Jack's eccentric sayings. I laughed out loud at some of the 'in-tents madness' and absurd situations that life throws at our protagonists. Very funny, and touching." **Laurita**

"A cautionary tale of how we could all slip through the cracks if we're not careful. A survival story told with great wit and humility. The book is also charmingly illustrated with line drawings that bring out the humour of the story?" **Distoviolin**

a
thought?

er →

Chapter 1.

It all started with a wink;

**"I'm a playful chestnut mare looking for a trusty,
lusty stallion to make me whinny again...."**

My profile: Where 'The Blue Eyed Man' and I met.

One problem though, Alex lived in the UK,

I lived in NZ!

!!! The other side of the friggin world !!!

We emailed for about three months and got to know
eachother inside out, not outside in.

I lived in Auckland with my son and had worked
across three continents as an advertising art
director.

I'd even won some shiny metal objects, the best
being a CANNES Silver Lion given for an 'Excita'
condom ad.

My son proudly took one (condom) to school for 'Show
and Tell!' That took some explaining.

These days, I clean bums including my own;/ \|

Leaving On A Jet Plane

We stood at Auckland airport, me clutching a one-way
ticket to London. It had all come about so fast,
my son was grown up and about to leave home. I was
about to go home after eighteen years. I passed
through customs with tears streaming down my face,
there was no turning back. The flight was spent in
a daze, I didn't want any wine/beer (v unusual).
I didn't watch any films (ditto). Instead spending
24hrs staring out of the round window thinking
about my old life, the one I'd left behind, hurtling
towards my new life at 570mph.

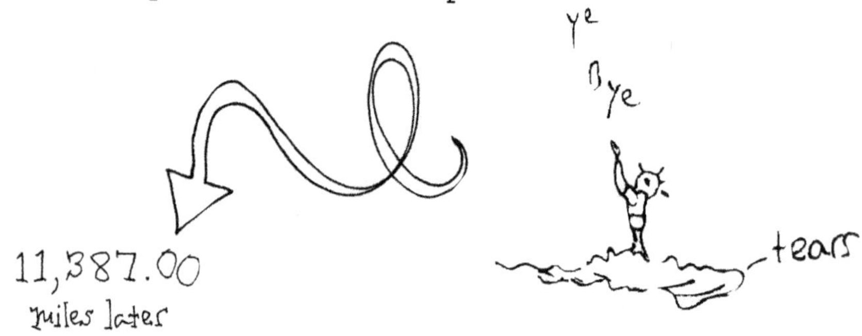

I'd meet Alex in real life, I'd seen some photos
but? I phoned him the next morning and was relieved
that:
  a) He sounded male.
b) Had broken his voice.
c) Didn't have an oooo arrr accent.

We arranged to meet later that day.

Two hours later I got into his car and he got into
mine (joke). We went to a pub in the village where
he lived. My mind was all over the place, not helped
by jetlag and six hours sleep in 48hrs.

**This is him. This is bloody HIM!! The guy I'd been
emailing for the past three months! Did I like what
I saw?? Was HE what I was expecting!!??**

At the pub I ordered a glass of Shiraz, the barwoman
said: "D'you want a small or a large glass?" What?
Cheeky mare. "I'll have both, thank you…"

After two or three I was feeling good and relaxed.
We spent the whole afternoon and evening talking
about all sorts of things and without any awkward
silences! He took me back to the train station,
I went to London where I'd arranged to stay with
Laura, my oldest and best-est friend.

I fully intended to move to London and carry
on working in advertising. I emailed Creative
Directors, even sent them a few pieces of my work.
No response?!! I should have used the phone or
hurled myself in front of them, "gis a job, I can do
it!"

But, I didn't and my life changed. Dramatically.
Suddenly I was Ms No Skills with No experience
trying to get a job in anything really.
CV = Over-qualified.
CV = Under-qualified in what I had applied for.

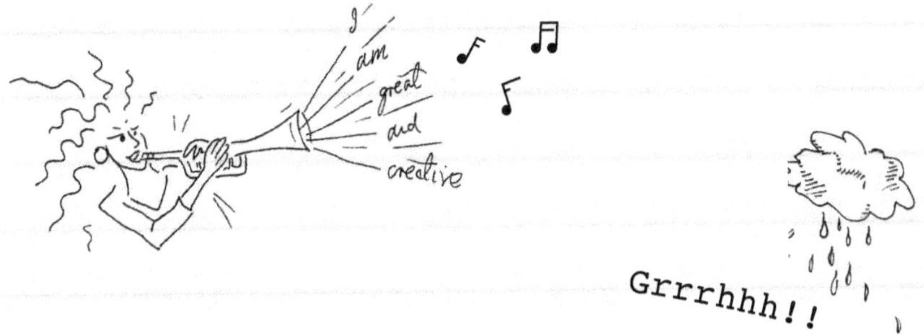

Dirty Weekends

The weekends were fantastic. We might stay in bed
the entire time with food, wine, DVD's and a fair
amount of nudge nudge, wink wink, here we go. We
laughed and talked about all sorts of things, but
sometimes nothing.

We'd watch the clouds sweep by becoming all sorts of
shapes like animals, dragons, cherubs, and……
wait, I hear violins in the background and other
Mills & Boon lovely stuff.

We drove into the New Forest or to the coast to get
our water fix, and visited villages mostly with a
local pub which we would always land up in!

Alex had a large garage with lots of 'manly' things,
like his work bench that ran the width of the
garage, neatly piled with tools, paint brushes and
other stuff. In the centre was a 125cc motorbike that
he was working on, innards cast on the floor.
He had a blue Triumph Tiger 1000cc lounging on one
side, ready to pounce into Europe in the better
weather.

That's enough about me (well, for the moment
anyway).OK, it's over to you Alex?

Alex: "I worked for Fastcrete as the Administration
and Workshop Manager at their head office."
He added: "Fastcrete supplies concrete finishing
equipment to the construction industry and ind…"

Me: "OK, that's enough Alex,
   this is my book…"

After about a year, I moved in with Alex. It was
happy, happy days.

During that time I needed to buy some wheels. How
many of you have been out bid right at the last
minute? Automatic bidding I think it's called.

Alex calls it something else.

We managed to win the bidding and it turned out to
be in a market town called Marlborough, not too far
from where we lived.

The previous owner was an Archeologist and the car
had been on television quite a few times.

My super star car is a blue convertible Suzuki
Vitara. We added big, wide alloy wheels and a
bullbar with extra headlights. It looks fantastic
and it's become a very loyal friend over the years.

Alex drove it onto his v large truck, strapped
it down, and made sure it was secure. I was duly
impressed, not having had this type of relationship
before.

Alex's first trip to NZ

My son was about to graduate from University and I wasn't going to miss it. The only job I could get was in domicilary care(r) pay = minimum wage, no experience needed!! My bank offered me a credit card, how could I say no?

Alex was keen to go as well, we decided to combine the graduation with a holiday which we spent touring around the north island.

He loved it! I loved it! We loved it!

After a few weeks of Do We, Don't We, Do We, Don't We, we whole-heartedly decided, YES!!! We WILL move back to NZ. I was a permanent resident and should be able to get Alex in as my partner. He started the application which meant finding an immigration lawyer in NZ.

The requirements were:
Proof that we were a couple, like letter's to us at our address, party invitations, Christmas cards.
A full Medical = £100.00
Blood Tests = £90.00
X-Ray = £100.00
Photos = £5.00
Immigration Lawyer = £1,500.00
Total = £1,795.00

We collected and sent everything off and waited to hear from Immigration New Zealand re: Working Visa for Alex.

SUPER
GiRL!

<u>Definition (noun)</u>

Domiciliary Care is a service provided
by the local Council that allows people
to remain in their home during later
life, whilst still receive assistance
with their personal care needs.

****

Hmmm, Whose Caring For Who?

I was at work, having a(nother) stressful moment at one of my domiciliary caring jobs.

INTERIOR. LAUNDRY ROOM — MORNING
I had taken the client's laundry downstairs to put into one of the washing machines. She was very particular about what machine it went in, being a bit of an old bag. I mildly panicked on my way down the stairs and couldn't remember which was the **wrong** machine and which was the **right** machine. After sliding money into the first machine and pressing START. OH SHIT! Wrong one.

****

The situation wasn't helped by a young female going up and down the long corridor at an alarming pace on two wooden sticks that she used as legs. She apologised when she shot past the laundry room as I asked repeatedly for help. ' I'm very sorry, very, very, very sorry indeed, put the money in, I'm very sorry, I'm very sorry, that machine, I'm very, very, very sorry, very sorry indeed…'

I felt a sudden burst of adrenaline, wrestled with the washing machine and got the money back and the door open. But it all took some time. As a carer, you're always racing against time. I rushed out and realised I had forgotten not only her floor, but also her flat no.

MY rota was in MY bag which was in HER flat.

"Bang, Bang I shot you down" started ringing and vibrating in my blue and white tunic pocket. I grabbed my phone at that (idiotic) moment, dropping washing powder all over the floor.

"I've got the work visa!!" Shouted Alex.

I shouted back, "That's greeeaaattt!!"

I resigned (thankfully) from domiciliary care.

Alex resigned from his job at Fastcrete where he had worked for thirteen years.

We started a new chapter of our lives in New Zealand.

We

were

b
  u
    z
      z
        i
          n
            g

! !

!

But, 7 Months Later

We returned from NZ utterly broke and broken hearted

"The person who makes
no mistakes does not
usually make anything"
— Edward John Phelps

Chapter 2.

Home Again, Home Again, Clippety Clop

In the UK once again we'd arranged to stay with my father in Wellington, Somerset.

Alex felt hopeful. I felt empty.

We caught a National Coach from Heathrow to Taunton, even the motorways seemed to be against us. M3 & M4 blocked with accidents/road works. We arrived at 11.00pm, three hours late. My father came and picked us up in his little Nissan Micra. He said, "I'm not sure I can fit all your luggage in!" It was all we owned.

We sat with bags and coats on our laps and suitcases in the boot. The car wobbled off.

Alex had pre-arranged his interview with a 'prestigious' car manufacturer @10.00am the following morning. He put on his Ted Baker suit, polished shoes, shirt and tie then we all left for Exeter. My father and I kept our fingers crossed in the car.

Five minutes later, Alex came out. The job at Jaguar had gone three days ago though it was unknown to the recruiter.

Here begins our story ›››

Oh, bollocking bollockingshit!!!!

We thought of the last forty-eight hours:

a. Selling our car in NZ for a huge loss.
b. Paying for flights on Alex's credit card, now almost maxed out.
c. Sodding job had already gone.

We should have done a million other things, except rush (stupidly) back.

I felt physically sick.

Alex sunk immediately into a deep anxiety/depression
which I'd never seen before. He looked suddenly old
and haunted as the pounds dropped off him. At times I
didn't even know him or what to say.

I kept asking myself...

What was wrong with what we had here?

Alex had a well-paid job.

I could have looked around for something better.

How could that happiness be
extinguished so completely?

What had happened to 'us?'

They

were

all

useless

questions

****

My superstar car needed to be put on the road, taxed
and insured. My credit card was maxed out. Alex
had enough money on his to pay for six months of
road tax and set me up with monthly payments for my
insurance. This became an additional nightmare.

We never had sex which hurt more than anything. Alex
had never experienced this feeling of nothingness
before. He tried to increase his bank loan as he'd
had been with them for the last forty years.
The bank said no. We lost our independence
completely as we moved in with my father, then my
mother and back with my father.

If that wasn't bad enough I received an email
from the New Zealand Council, inviting me for an
interview.

Alex would get calls three times a day from the bank
about his credit card or loan, they were mostly
electronic messages and not calls from a person.
I hated them for the way they made Alex feel. Stupid
and worthless.

And, if you did get a person they wouldn't be from
this country.

"IT'S DOING THE UK PEOPLE OUT OF A JOB!!!" shouts
the old and loved Alex!! "I know, I know, get off
your soapbox will you!"

We signed on the dole, a depressing task. They
advised us to sign on as a couple.

SO WE DID...

Alex landed a job at another prestigious car manufacturer in Barnstable. Therefore I got nothing. You hear about people using and abusing the system, I don't know how. Alex was spending lots on fuel and had taken a large drop in salary. He was traveling an hour there, an hour back, starting at seven thirty, finishing at six thirty, six days a week.

He loathed it. We couldn't move to Barnstable as we couldn't afford the deposit, rent in advance, letting fee etc. This came to to about four grand.

It makes you wonder if you're better off not having a job rather than working on a very low salary, paying emergency tax, and a job you can't survive on!

Alex handed his notice in as he couldn't afford to commute there on his salary. His recruiter was pissed off, they had most of the jobs in the car/ transport industry. We were well and truly screwed.

Alex managed to get a temporary job fixing motorbikes in a workshop, which was word of mouth and cash in hand. He absolutely refused to sign on the dole again...ever!

It was very hard to actually earn any money without having money in the first place. Even the supermarkets are onto it. It's cheaper to buy three products than one. But, if you can only afford one, you get screwed as it's more expensive to buy one than three. The rich get richer, the poor get poorer.

It felt like an invisible hand releasing you,
allowing you to take a few wobbly steps and then
slamming you back again, even further than before.
Our feelings, dreams, ourselves were being toyed
with, our lives complete public knowledge.

"How are you getting on?" "Have you got a job yet?"
"Are you still looking for a job because so and so
are looking?" "Haven't you found anything yet?"

"WHY DON'T YOU JUST FUCK OFFFF!!"

I got a job as a support worker. It sounds better
than a carer but it's pretty much the same thing.
I had to do lots of e-learning before starting work
+ waiting for my DBS, which took a long time as I've
moved around in the last five years a fair bit.

We moved in with my mother who has six children. Can
you imagine! Four from my father and two more from
her second marriage.

My mother lives in a big house that's been in my
stepfather's family for generations, but it's
dilapidated in parts. She said that we could do up
the attic with a view to living in it. We were super
excited, and set to work right away thinking that
this could be our home.

We cleaned and cleared out what would be our
bedroom, painted the walls and stripped back the
oak beams. We did up the sitting room, hiring a floor
plainer and then varnished, so the floors looked
amazing.

Our new neighbours we're bats and large spiders, who
were interested in what we were doing up there.
Then all of a sudden, it was taken away. It proved

to be something that was hard to get over between my mother and I, as we're usually close.

But, I felt sickened.

We moved back in with my father.

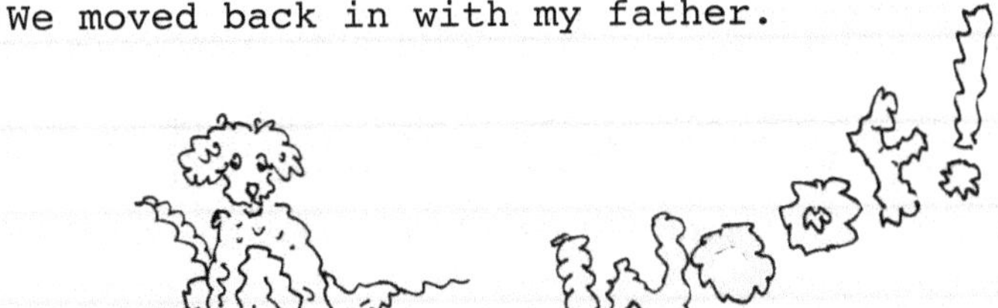

Finally, my DBS came through and I completed my e-learning and started work as bank staff in Bristol. I used to work long days or nights, sometimes both as it was quite a way to drive. It must be said, my superstar car is a secret petrol guzzler.

I had my first experience in LD, (Learning Disability).

I never thought I would like it having had a brief experience in my sixth form, when walking into town when I came across some young men with Downs. I must have fondly looked over being safely on the other side of the road when they started shouting "Get your knickers off...get your knickers off" amid chortles of laughter.

Anna was in her early twenties and had Downs, with schitzophrenia. She had a full rucksack that she would frequently hit and shout at. I never saw what was inside it but was intrigued. It looked roughly the size of a support worker's head! Anna shared a flat with Paul, who was about her age. He would crawl around, pulling himself up on various objects. His all time favourite thing was his radio his all time favourite sound was having it between stations, ppppppsssspppppssssssstttt…!!! And, he liked it really, really, really LOUDDD…!! On the first night when it was Paul's bedtime I went in to his bedroom and switched off the stereo as it said to do in his support plan.

I tried to entice him to go to bed, but he wasn't having any of it. I turned off the light and shut the door.

Suddenly, I heard all this noise from his room but thought nothing of it as it stopped after about 10 mins.

The next morning, I knocked on his door and tried to go in. It turned out that he had put his bed against the door, barricading me out!!

I thought, **I like you.**

Alex hated it when he wasn't working so he would line up cash in hand jobs for the coming weeks. One of his friends was a workshop manager in Southampton who needed holiday cover for one of his mechanics. He couldn't say no and meant he stayed in Southampton during the week, with a friend and would come back for weekends. It wasn't ideal as things between us still weren't that great.

I subsidised my Bristol work with a local job,
cooking for a woman called Joan with early Dementia.
Her son Paul was around a great deal and was her
main carer.

I liked him and the three of us had a good laugh.

Joan used to fart all the time, she couldn't help
it…! "I'm very sorry…" clasping the back of her
skirt. "Oooh, I'm so sorry…" "…Oooh, excuse me……"
as the farts were getting louder the more she moved
across the room!!

My job was to cook her lunch from scratch. Joan was
not that keen on food and would pass things to her
greedy dog, Buttercup, if she thought no-one was
watching. Joan would sometimes blame her farts on
Buttercup.

Buttercup

Buttercup sat next to her, watching every mouthful. The greedy dogs diet(GDD) was:

Breakfast: Scrambled free-range eggs with some dog supplements sprinkled on top.

Dinner: Lots of freshly cooked vegetables by yours truly, dog biscuits, cooked chicken (courtesy of Paul), or sardines in oil.

I used to leave Buttercup's tea on the side when I left at 1.30 with one of Paul's notes:

"BUTTERCUP'S TEA, GIVE AT 5.30"
+ Paul used to leave other notes all around the house, like EVENING PILLS, by her bedside. She had notes in the fridge, JOAN'S TEA AT 6 O'CLOCK… PAUL'S NUMBER…

Buttercup used to take advantage of Joan's dementia. As soon as I had gone, she would stand in the kitchen, looking at her dinner on the counter and then Joan, dinner, Joan, dinner, Joan. She would give it to her way before dinner time as Joan was a little obsessive about feeding her and couldn't remember if she had fed her or not. Eventually, I had to hide Buttercup's dinner in a disused fridge and give it to her myself as she was getting fatter and fatter.

Mostly these notes worked well, but she got a lot worse quite quickly and eventually needed 24 hr care.

Meanwhile…

***

Carer To Career

I'm one of the advertising art directors on a
Dutch agency in Amsterdam that hadn't come up with
anything to date, but suddenly IT DID!

I was to fly to Tunisia to work on a pitch for ten
days.

Now? Oh, shit!!

Alex offered to make Joan and Buttercup meals until
I was back again.

Was the hotel paid for? What about transport?
Plane tickets? Insurance? My card was maxed out,
I had about twenty pounds to my name. I tried
calling my credit card and getting them to increase
my limit?
I was told a BIG FAT NO! In fact the credit card
person seemed to think I was possibly quite mad and
probably lying about the whole trip.

My father lent me £500 and everything was paid for
by the advertising agency. I had to go there for
myself!
One minute you're on the bread line, counting
pennies, looking in coats, jeans for a forgotten
pound (if you're lucky). Next moment I'm kissing
Alex 'Goodbye...' at Bristol airport and flying
business class.

I was suddenly the dogs Doodahs.

Oh, the extremes of life!!

My time in Tunisia was hard work with no days off.
Not speaking very good French was another major
problem.

When I arrived I was picked up by a chauffeur and
taken straight to work even though it was 9.30pm.
I was briefed by this incredibly good looking CD,
who owned not only this agency but all it's off
shoots in the middle east.

I thought, Wow!!

I was taken to the hotel which was out of this world. There were Persian rugs everywhere, the largest four-poster bed I had ever seen. The bathroom was huge, tiled in an intricate, beautiful pattern, the floors were smoky marble.

But, I didn't see a lot of my room because we all worked from 8.00am — 10.30pm. I was lucky enough to be paid per hour outside my standard day rate. I called Alex every night via skype, it was good for me as it was my dose of reality. Still, after a shaky start I did some nice ideas for Tunisian small businesses.

See below.

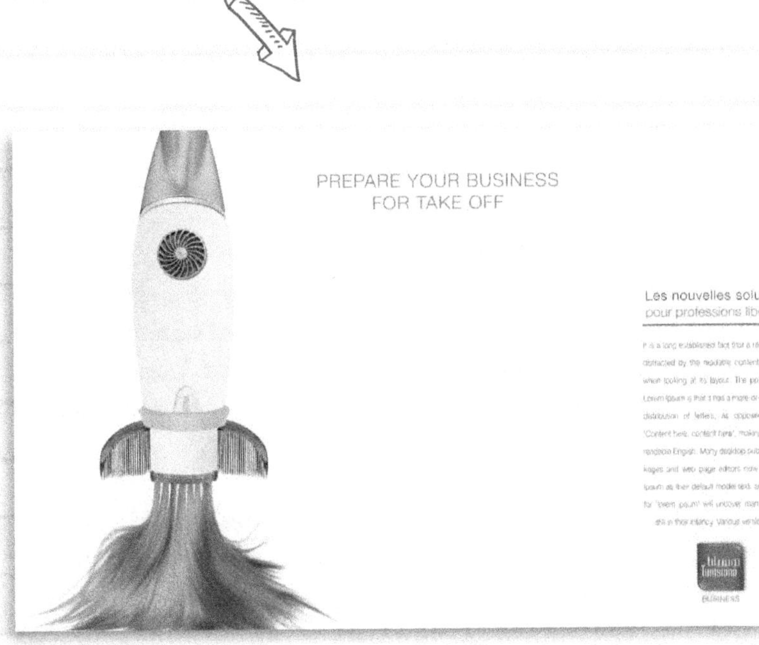

The whole trip did a lot for my confidence and I believed in myself again. I was more sure of my relationship with Alex, and where I fitted into the world.

We were suddenly able to have a plan, a future based on this money. We both wanted to move back to the Wiltshire area. We did move, but back in with my father again.

The Dutch agency who handled the Tunisian trip still hadn't been paid, so they couldn't pay me.

What, why?

Training at Mr Crutch!

Alex had an interview at Mr Crutch as a manager in their Portsmouth branch. He hadn't heard back from them. It's pretty crap not to hear back but happened to us quite a few times!

We were sharing a very rare pint in the local pub when we got talking to the landlord and landlady! Alex said that he was looking for a job, she said she'd have a word with a regular who was looking for someone to help out.

The job was for a driver, picking up vegetables
@ 5am, finishing at lunchtime.
Pay = Minimum Wage.
But, it was a job. The hours were shit and Alex
wouldn't earn enough for us to move out of my
father's house, after paying off the dreaded loan and
so on.

But, he got a call from Mr Crutch as we were doing
our daily walk/exercise/privacy around Wellington
Monument.

He had got the job!!

Excellent news we thought...

We went back to our dilemma:

Driving job = no money, but very nice
guy.
But have to go on living with my father.
OR
Mr Crutch = Opportunity?
In Portsmouth, better salary,
independence, life back.

Money won hands down, always the case.
Alex had to go on a training course in Crawley for
the next two weeks, and we'd stay in a hotel? This
posed the question of money, petrol and the hotel
bill.

Never underestimate money, without it you're well
and truly screwed.   What to do?

I emailed the Dutch Agency and asked for an advance on the Tunisian money? They said no as they STILL hadn't been paid. What?? I worked in Tunisia about 3 months ago. What's going on? As luck would have it (very rare in our present lives) I got a letter from the tax office. What was more amazing, I opened it. It turned out that it was a tax rebate for £480.00!

We speedily packed our bags, kissed my father goodbye, filled up with petrol and drove to Crawley. The hotel was cheap, twenty-pounds a night and Alex would be able to claim it back. There was no way we could afford to eat at the hotel, so went to the co-op instead and hid bread, hummus, cheese, salad and sometimes a bottle of wine under our sweaters! We brought some plastic knives and plates with us, the coffee and tea was included in the hotel price. I should mention that it was snowing at the time, so cold food wasn't ideal.

While Alex was off doing his training, I spent the majority of the day either:

a. Applying for jobs in Salisbury/Southampton/ Portsmouth.
b. In the hot and bubbly bath.
c. On the free internet in reception (which was next to the restaurant selling loads of HOT FOOD!!)

I would hungrily watch people eat. I think it's terrible how so many people waste food, I felt like rooting through the bins but managed to hold off.

We were hungry for hot food and dying for a beer, or a glass of wine. Alex wasn't enjoying the job and didn't get along with the other manager. He sounded very full of himself, downright unpleasant.

Two weeks later, we dubiously drove back down to
Wellington. Alex couldn't say no to Mr Crutch and we
had hopes of moving back to the Wiltshire area.

Alex started this coming Monday. We were racking
our 'brains' (somehow, it didn't feel like that) as
to how we would cope with nowhere to stay and very
little money for petrol/food etc.

"The trouble with the rat race is that
even if you win, you're still a rat."
– Lily Tomlin

A caravan?

We spoke to an elderly relative about using his
caravan which was in storage. He agreed to it.
We thought GREAT!!! Freedom at last!

It cost us a round of coffee and cakes. Coffee and
cakes are so expensive? Especially x 5.

But oddly enough the caravan didn't materialise,
although we asked again and again. I even offered to
buy it when I got paid from Tunisia.

We didn't even see it.

In-tents Madness

"Well," Alex volunteered, "We might not have a caravan but we do have a 2-man tent."

"Well, OK then," I said.

There was a campsite, half way between Portsmouth and Salisbury. That was good for me as I had organised some support work.

Before we went my father bought us a camping stove, kettle, some tins of food, a saucepan, some coffee, milk, a torch and bid us goodbye thinking that they must be completely insane.

We set off on this venture. Alex went first with me following behind in my trusty, lusty, superstar car.

I noticed a fair amount of snow as we got over the border into Wiltshire.
My spirits dropped somewhat, but I thought, "I'm into this!! Independence!! Yay!!"

We pulled into the campsite which was completely deserted apart from the odd caravan. There was a number to call in the office window.

The campsite manager walked briskly to her office.

Alex caught her up: "Hiya, we've got a small 2-man tent, we'd like to camp here for the week?"

Her eyes said:

"Are you completely off your rocker…?!!

Our eyes said:

"Yes … I think we probably are!" But, needs must.

The view from the office showed ice on the duck pond, four inches of snow on the campsite.

I wondered if she'd mind if we stayed here as it was warm and comfortable. We could have joined her cat lounging on a shelf, right above the heater! I stared menacingly at it. It stared back, lazily yawning.

***

The manager disappeared behind her booking desk and suddenly looked professional as she took her diary out and got to work with her pen. We were put on a site underneath trees bordering the bathrooms.

She added that all the bathrooms had heated floors.
Oh, Yes!
And was open 24hrs.
Double Oh, Yes!

We, (OK Alex) put the tent up at four o'clock. It got dark at 4.30, the only lighting we had was from a very weak torch.

He quickly blew up the lilo bed. Five minutes later we were in it. It was 4.45pm.

Alex and I thought positively, this wasn't bad at all!! No problem. But, I did look enviously at the few caravans parked there.

Bedtime.

Alex can go to sleep instantly and at any time. I can't. Still, we both had an unsettled, cold and sleepless night. At first daylight, we gazed at all the condensation inside the tent, all the dampness on the sleeping bags and on our fully clothed bodies.

Suddenly, we heard a loud screeeeeeeeeeching coming from outside the tent, " What's that??"
I whispered to Alex thinking that somehow we'd been transported to a wild life park!
I gingerly put my head out!

***

It turned out to be lots of geese jumping around aggressively, probably complaining about the ice on the pond. I hoped they wouldn't do that every day, I preferred the more sedate cock-a-doodle-do which was annoying enough!! I crawled out first and stretched my aching body. I grabbed my make-up and disappeared to the bathroom, throwing myself down on to the heated floor to get the true benefit. I was cold right through, to the bone(s). After washing my face, brushing my hair, I cleaned my teeth and then set about putting my face on. Lipstick last, for courage. I ventured outside feeling a bit more normal and saw Alex who was out of the tent by now.

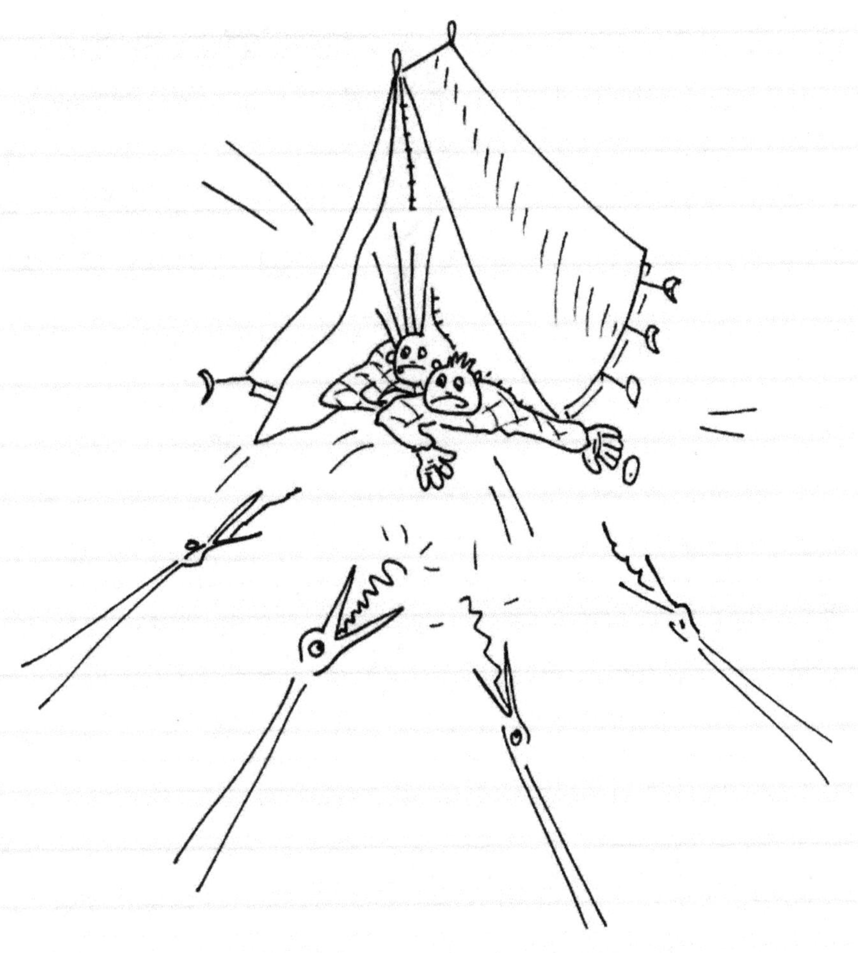

He said:

"This isn't going to work"

I said:

Oh, I should mention that I was 50 and he was 59.

He phoned his new boss and was given seven days to sort himself out or……
We turned around and went back in two cars, back to my father's house. AGAIN.

I seriously think I would have followed him over a cliff, like that great scene in Thelma and Louise!

SURVIVAL = 12 HOURS!!

Things we learnt:

a. Camping in winter was never going to work, as much as we wanted it to.

b. It made us more determined to try again.

"youth is wasted on the young."
— Oscar Wilde / George Bernhard Shaw

Motor Bike = Caravan

Alex traded in his Triumph Tiger 1000cc when we first came back from NZ, trying to keep the bank off his back.

He now owned a 1200cc Suzuki Bandit. It would be worth around £2,000.00 as it had low mileage and was in top condition.

We should have £1,500.00 to spend on a caravan.

Caravan's were much more that that, even for a shitty one. The first caravan we looked at was certainly that.

It had about twenty-five dead flies trapped in between the window's double-glazing.

But, it was £1,500.00.

The sales man was smarmy. We looked at each other and said, "Nope! We can't live with twenty-five dead flies trapped in the window."

We looked on e-bay for static caravans that would give us independence. It turned out that the campsite was way more expensive than the static.

We found a houseboat in the Southampton area. Crazy, crazy excitement about this new venture!!!! Alex phoned up the owner and got lots more pictures. But, it turned out that the mooring was more expensive than the boat. We couldn't afford to do any of the work bearing in mind that it needed to be taken out of the water, painted and done up. This would be very expensive.
I can just see us, living in a boat but in a field somewhere!

Our spirits dropped.

Back to e-bay again. We looked for caravans in the Somerset area and found one very close to my father's address. It looked clean and was the right price.

We went to see it.

It was a great little caravan, little being the operative word! But we liked it, when he added that there was an almost new awning included in the price and it would be sold with lots of tools, gas bottle, cutlery etc. We thought, 'Yeah, this'll work…' Only problem was Alex hadn't put his bike on eBay yet.

He held it for us for one day.

On the way back to my fathers place, we got talking again. Maybe Alex's motorbike wouldn't sell straightaway, or, it might not sell at all.

We told my father about the caravan, he asked to see it. He had a good look around it and then, all of a sudden,

lent us

the money

to buy it..!!

HAPPY

My Father was incredibly happy with having us to stay and all his neighbours knew exactly what had happened to us, keeping up to date with all our dramas, job hunts etc. I'm sure all of Somerset knew. He knew that we needed to be independent again, that was his way of letting go…!!

Thank you.

Still one problem, we didn't have a towing vehicle?

As my father handed over the cheque, Bill and Sarah mentioned that they were going to see their daughter in Southampton.

Hey wait a minute, Southampton is very close to the campsite. Deep breath from me ...

"Do you think you could tow the caravan to the campsite, it's not that far from Southampton?"

They laughed and said, "No problem."

So, the next day our party left. Alex in his car, me in mine and lastly but not least-ly, the X-trail towing OUR caravan. We went back to the same campsite. Bill and Sarah helped us to put up the awning. That was a great addition and bigger than the whole caravan. When they left, I was excitedly going through all the features of our new home. I opened the fridge and saw a decorative paper bag. Inside was a bottle of wine with a card from Bill and Sarah…

'Welcome to your new home!!'

We put the bike on eBay for £2,000.00. It sold in about five minutes.

All is good/good is GREAT!!

Calculations:
Motorbike = £2,000.00
Owed = £1,500.00
     = Not enough

My father kindly accepted £1,000.00, leaving us with £1,000.00 to survive a month on until we were paid.

Expenses were:
Campsite rent £80.00 p/w = £320.00 p/m
Electricity £10.00 p/w = £40.00 p/m
Petrol = A huge amount
Alex = 70 mls a day
Kate = 30 mls a day
Surplus: Car expenses. Road tax. Insurance.
PLUS Food.

Chapter 3.

Greenhill Farm Caravan Park

The caravan was ***** star! It was our independence,
and really did save our lives and relationship.

But, it put more pressures on our plate, for
instance:

a. Alex's job at Mr Crutch wasn't going that well.
b. I didn't have full time work.
c. We were living on the breadline, but still beyond
   our means.
d. We were running two cars to get to work.
   Nightmare.
e. We got behind on our campsite rent because of d.
   It's very hard to catch up if get behind on rent
   or anything else essential.

It was about this time Alex had a bad-ass toothache.
We tried all the usual ways to take the pain away
like pliers (joking) but he was almost at that
stage.

We didn't have enough money for him to see/get it
taken out by the Dentist. He endured the pain, and
kept smiling!

Whatttt!!!! Smiling!!!! I remember him as being in
total agony.

Alex went to A&E, explained briefly that he didn't
have a dentist and asked for anti-biotics. As soon
as he started the course, the gum calmed down.
Eventually, the tooth became so loose that while he
was driving along the motorway he prodded/pushed
and pulled, whoooooooosh out it came!! to his great
relief.

I asked him where he put it, thinking that I might
sell it on ebay. Said he put it in the glove box and
then in the bin. Damnnn!!

"Teeth are like stars, they come out at night!!"

— Captain Jack*

But on the + side the campsite was beautiful and in
the heart of the New Forest. There were spacious
loos, shower blocks, two washing machines, two
dryers all with heated floors!

Geese and ducks lived by the picturesque pond,
they were very tame and lived quite happily on
breadcrumbs.

In the morning, or when we came home, the
ducks would race over to our awning making a
quaaaaaaaaaaaaacking noise of great excitement. In
the summer we sat on fold out camping chairs next
to the pond, reading, or talking. The ducks sat
clucking contentedly in our shadow.

I read an article some years ago saying that white
breadcrumbs are very bad for a ducks insides! I had
a go at making what was recommended, which took
ages. It consisted of bran and other healthy
ingredients, which I have now forgotten. The ducks
hated it and disappeared in disgust leaving all the
food floating briefly before sinking like a bad dream.
These days, we give them brown bread crumbs, which
is hopefully better.

* **Alex's father was a retired army officer whose funny
  sayings stay with Alex and are spread throughout this
  book.**

The geese were slightly different. They were too
big and pushy for me and had an unpleasant beak
that opened, hisssssssssssssssss-ed with a snake
like tongue flicking.They would flap their wings
with neck and body stretched as they ran at you,
feathers puffed out in order to show who was boss.
It worked on me! There was one male that thought it
should live in our awning, he was forever trying to
barge in. I was scared of him but held my ground
firmly with the zip-up doorway around me, closing it
quickly behind.

There was a cat on the campsite. It was a very
friendly, dark brown Burman-esque creature that
tried to get into our awning and succeeded a few
times.

I don't quite know what it is about our awning?!!

We threw it out nicely, but firmly.

We had just treated ourselves to a duvet cover with
pillow cases and a sheet from tkmaxx. They were
the height of luxury. We had been sleeping inside a
double sleeping bag which was rough and bobbly and
not terribly clean with duvet inner on top, plus
two of my fathers dog blankets. A few weeks later
we washed all of our bed linen for the first time,
leaving it on the air-er outside while we went for
a walk. Later, we took all the bed linen in and
the whole lot stank of cat spray!! Almost the worst
smell in the world.

The cat was watching from a distance! I should say, a safe distance!

Alex was plotting his revenge. It varied between killing the cat and killing the little fucker…!!!

He strung up a washing line between two trees, out of cat height.

The caravan was our home. But at times, we would have to remind ourselves that this was Our Home as we'd been homeless for so long. It didn't matter that the caravan was twenty years old or how big or small it was, we just made it as nice as it could be.

Let's go inside…

There were two long sofas with a small chest of drawers in between. You were able to hook the table(s) at the top. The base of the lower drawer had a pull out wooden, slatted base for a double bed. You turned the cushions the other way, they had a mattress backing.

Ingenious!

There was a kitchen at the other end. It had a small gas stove/oven, fridge and a sink that was below another worktop. There was lots of cupboards/ storage, and everything was held in place so that you could, Hit The Road, Jack!! Never Coming Back, No More, No More, No More, No More…
Well, that's if you have a towing vehicle, which we didn't.

There was a minute bathroom with a shower. I couldn't figure out where the sink was, but it was very neatly designed and became part of the wall when you weren't using it. You could hear all the sink water rushing into the wastewater and that made one feel intensely satisfied. But, one day it rushed onto the bathroom floor, and soaked everything. Alex took the sink off the wall and put his investigative arm right in the cold, scummy water, looking for the culprit. A bar of soap!

I suppose it could have been a lot worse, like a rat or something...!

We'd never used the shower, partly due to the fact that you couldn't swing a cat inside it was that small, and couldn't really compete with the showers on site, with their lovely heated floors. We used it as another storage area. It's a good thing that we're both small.
When I was about six, I had a book about a goblin/ elf who had his entire home inside a shoe. Well, it was sort of like that, except I had out grown my goblin phase. Alex was a bit elflike!

There was an electric hook up for the small plot of
gravelled campsite that we paid for in our rent.
It was in an ideal place as it backed onto a field,
separated by a tree-lined stream, near the outward
barrier, close to the bathrooms and septic tank
wastage area.

There are certain things you're supposed to do when
living in a caravan, like emptying the loo on a
daily basis, filling up the loo flusher with water.
We couldn't afford the chemicals that were supposed
to go down the loo. It meant that all un-speakables
had to be done in the campsite loo, not that I would
have done one in the caravan loo anyway.

It's a very basic life where you can't take anything
for granted. Attempting to flush the loo when you've
run out of water, or the dial on the loo is red
which means it's very full! This could send the
contents straight back up, and over the loo, making
a nasty smelling flood!

We'd try to empty the wastewater daily. I've no idea
why it smelt so much if you didn't?

The eight-gallon tank of drinking water would run
out quite regularly, always when you're in a hurry
and about to spit toothpaste, or shave.
And that's just me, ha ha.

There was a very neat appliance for rolling the
water from the caravan to the drinking water tap.
Only problem being that you had to lift the full tub
down off the step under the tap, without spilling/
upturning it. Good for the arm muscles!

I said daily, but it never worked like that.
Sometimes, it was the last thing we wanted to do,
especially in winter.

I mentioned that we had an awning. It was like an
extension to the caravan and made of tent like
material with windows all around.

We used that as a lounge and put the larger table
out there and had two camping chairs either side.
The problem with camping chairs is that at first they
support you in every way. But pretty soon, the legs
start to slowly collapse and you are left, almost
lying down, groping for food, drink, knife and fork
off the table.

We had a conservatory sofa and chair, iron and
ironing board and that was about it. We used the
awning's central pole to hang all our laundered
clothes, which made it look and smell something like
a Chinese laundry! We ate there in summer, plus
unzipped the windows as we got the sun first thing in
the morning. Good for our tans.

Alex put pallets on the awning floor to keep it
warmer in winter, as the air could circulate
underneath. We were going to put bales of straw
underneath the caravan but the idea of rats put us
off.

After nearly being poisoned by carbon monoxide, we
stopped using the gas heater. All I remember is
lying on the bed one minute and getting seriously
dizzy the next. Then I crawled out through the
caravan door and fell safely into our awning where i
lay for about ten minutes with stars and stripes and
horrible rushing noises in my head.

Alex had a sort of faint in the tiny bathroom. I
thought omg how am i ever going to get you out of
there! He tried to stand up but his legs buckled
under him, I got him to crawl over and into bed. He
was fine a few minutes later. I just think it was the
strain of everything that was going on in our lives
at that time.

In winter, we left the bed up during the week. If
it was freezing we ate in bed, electric blanket on
full, (my present a few years ago to Alex) sitting
either side of our tiny, built in chest of drawers
which we used as a table.

It was very comfortable and always smelt of the
spicy stir fries that we'd had at supper, one of my
specialty's.

OUR MEN'U

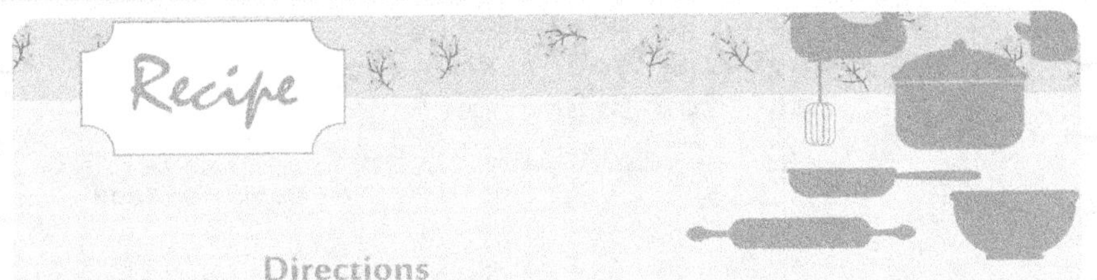

Directions

Ingredients

Stir fry: Use a well seasoned wok + 2 people.

Cut everything in bite size pieces.
Cook the onion in vegetable oil, garlic, chilli and ginger first. Then add the chopped up chicken/tofu/prawns/eggs. Add Soy, and keep adding all the vegetables. Lastly add some of the Oyster Sauce/Hoy Sin. Serve with rice.

Place the Wok on a wooden chopping board, in the middle of the table. Stuff your face!

We were lucky to have a farm shop in the village. It was a lot cheaper than the supermarket and fresher vegs.

Shallots

Celery

Parsnips

Any green vegetable like Pak Choy, green beans

Mushrooms

Peppers: Red, Green, Orange, Red

Either Chicken/Prawns/ Tofu

Bean Sprouts/ Baby Sweetcorn

Lots of Garlic

Lots of Chilli

Lots of fresh ginger

Dark Soy and Oyster Sauce/Hoy Sin

Lime

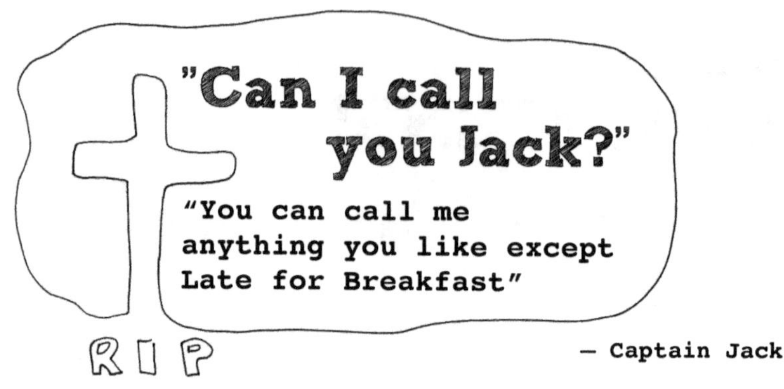

We have porridge for breakfast, which means getting up extra early, but it's worth it. Some people make porridge with milk, I make mine with water, it's nicer and cheaper. It provided a cheap and nutritious breakfast.

Fact: Porridge is good for cholesterol. I think it cleans out your veins or something + also protects against some cancers.

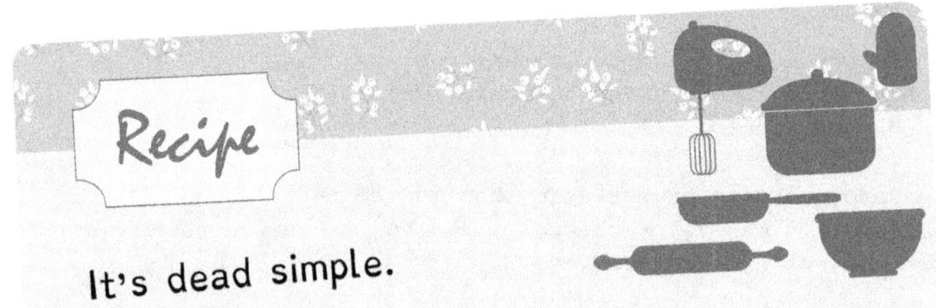

Empty a cup of water for each person, into a saucepan, use half that measure with oats, and bring to the boil stirring like a madman.
The oats will expand, and within 3-5 mins it's ready to put into bowls. We put honey in ours, and add a little milk.

"Up there for thinking, down there for dancing."

— Captain Jack

My father came to stay which was nice. He brought his two dogs with him. They had two eyes between them, long story!! He checked into a B&B, leaving the dogs with us. Poor dogs were used to central heating, we had none of that. My father told the B&B all about us and I'm talking ALL. Laura came twice in the summer she stayed at the B&B and heard all about us too. She loved the campsite and our new life as Romanies. It made her laugh the way the ducks followed us everywhere quack-quacking. Otherwise, we lost ourselves in books.

There was an amazing bookshop in Salisbury with a good selection of new books for £2.00. They sold second hand books in the basement so we could read one, then take it downstairs, get some money off the one we were going to buy = £1.00. Or sometimes, we would just swap them.

Play that Funky Music Loud Boy

Now and again we had a great day with music, food, a very rare bottle of wine and lots of loving.

Dressed in thick, hideous dressing gowns, socks, wellies, glass of wine in hand, candles, swaying to the music, enjoying the moment. You didn't know what pressures there would be tomorrow, but it wasn't hard to guess!

1, 2, 3 ...

Blow (51) Candles Out!

My son lives in Sydney, and for my birthday he sent me seven pairs of Bond's pants. I've worn them for years in NZ (not the same pair) but at that time you couldn't get them in the UK.

I went running up to our local Post Office to get my parcel. He had put the true value on them for customs, the Post Office said I had to pay import tax of £20.00 before I could receive the parcel!!! I was pretty close to tears when I heard that hating the cow sitting fatly behind the PO Counter, giving me a patronising looooook.

Unfortunately (fortunately for her) I couldn't lean across grab her by the throat and take my parcel as she was protected by glass. She added she would keep the parcel for two weeks and then 'return to the sender'.

I ran off.
TO GET MY BASE BALL BAT!!

Alex To The Rescue

It was summer, Alex was between jobs and doing
things outside like painting, gardening, working on
cars for cash in hand.

My car can do 200mls on one tank (milometer has
always been broken). It was on 216mls. I didn't have
any credit on my phone or in my bank account.

Panic, Panic

I was doing a course and had to drive all the way
there, which was much further than I thought! Worse
still a guy I worked with had asked for a lift
back. "Yes, you can have a lift, but you'll have to
buy some petrol first?" I didn't say that but I did
borrow his phone to call Alex.

Shit!! I was living a teenager's life.

Alex told me to try and get to the closest petrol
station. I was hoping and praying that I wouldn't
run out of petrol on the ring road. It's a fast
road.

What would I say? Sorry Police officer, I seem to
have run out of fuel, and (whispered) ...

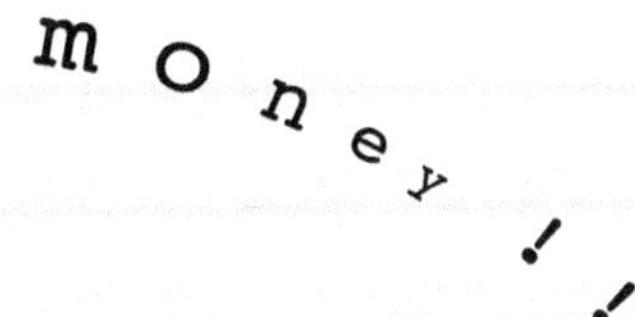

I did manage to get to a service station and waited
for Alex who put £10 in my tank. My car has been
a good friend to me. It appears to run on air and
promises!
When it finally dies (not yet I hope) we'll play "Love
Kills" by Queen, as we lower it down into it's final
resting place!

The fuel for Alex's and my commute was shocking,
Alex had to go further than me. He would put £10 in
his tank, it would only last one return trip as the
motorway was congested all the way.

We used to turn off our engines in heavy traffic and
dread the low petrol warning light. When that comes
on you know that you've got about 30 miles to find a
petrol station. Alex's light would come on twice a
day, it was incredibly depressing and kept going on
a wing and a prayer. We couldn't afford to tax and
MOT the cars. My big dread was:

a. The police
b. Accident
c. Running out of petrol

The police were quite fond of hiding in a lay-by on
the Southampton Rd, they can instantly tell if you
have tax or not.

Learning Disability

I was working in a day centre which I really enjoyed and had recently been employed full-time.
I would have to wait four weeks for my salary, not weekly like I had. But, on the other hand,
I had guaranteed work if I survived.

!!!No cash for a month!!!

I didn't know if I'd have enough petrol to get to work and back. Found out about the bus which was more expensive + I'd have to leave at about 5 am to guarantee getting there in time.

STILL...

I met people like Brittany, who grabbed my hair and wouldn't let go as she bounced along, dragging you behind. And she was just a support worker. Joke!

Molly used to laugh hysterically, usually with a paint-brush in hand, which she would throw at the wall amid even more giggles. She liked the ball pool and would bury herself in there giggling like anything. She pulled out a (feeding) peg from Simon's stomach. John would suddenly appear from behind, drawing his head backwards and forwards in a threatening way, until you shouted "STOP" and stood up. Then he would disappear, all six foot two of him speedily into the garden, usually with a plastic toy wrapped in his strapping fist.

Minnie would attack with her great chuckle, pulling
you down to wrestle with her. Paul would leap on you
and try to get on your shoulders.

Meanwhile, Ricky would shout from his wheelchair,
"Doooor Beeell" "Doooor Beeell." He liked it when
you drew stuff like disco lights, or Mr Dosworld's
blue sweater, Mr Oakfield's new trousers, a sausage
on a fork with ketchup or, chaaains!! Dan would
pretend to hit his forehead on the door by kicking
his boot on it first and then roar with laughter.
Lisa would self-harm, unless you were in range which
was definitely not a good place to be. I got a thump
in my stomach like that. You quickly learnt how to
tackle them. Or else!!!

MOT — Ministry Of T-bags

The next drama was, getting my car through it's MOT.
It failed due to needing extensive welding
underneath.

Alex got a quote, which was mate's rates but
still £500.00...! Oh no!! Sometimes you just felt
exhausted, up, down, up, down, up, down. Still no
money from Tunisia, it's going to court now. I asked
again for an advance? Told no. Sometimes, I wanted
to throw my head back and shout at the top of my
voice… "Oh, Fuck It, Fuck the Whole Fucking Lot of
You Fucking Fuckers…"

Alex had a few months work in Southampton which was
great, he had to drive me to work in Salisbury until
he got my car through it's MOT.

Mirror Mirror On The Wall

We Get Up And Then We Fall

We made an effort to look good and be cheerful.
There was no way we wanted people to see all the
struggle and tension on our faces. Alex would iron
his shirts, trousers in the awning on Sunday night
for the week ahead. He would shave every morning,
in the little mirror above the sink whatever job he
was doing. The razor blade was nine months old and
didn't shave very well at all. He tried disposable
razor blades, but they were worse. He grew a beard
and clipped it with a razor blade so it wasn't too
long and thick. He (kindly) gave me his old razor. I
used it on my legs but never on my face.

I was dressed ok too, thank you tkmaxx. I've picked
up nice clothes for three or four pounds, on the
clearance racks. Otherwise, I've got clothes from
ten/fifteen years ago. People still say they're
great!

Hmmnnn, really...??

Alex cleaned the caravan carpet with some industrial
stuff that he was given. It made a huge difference and
that was the end of wearing wellies/boots in the
caravan. Slippers or else!!!

Alex had some nasty grey sock ones that were given
as a present. I had some bright pink Indian slippers
given by Laura, which were very nice!

We called them Our Dorothy's @ the wizard of oz.
Alex would sometimes steal them, but, I must admit,
he looked good in them too ;p

Windy Winter

It's no fun battling your way to the showers in
winter, wearing only a dressing gown which you're
trying hard not to do a 'Marilyn in the Subway' and
Alex's wellies. A Tesco carrier bag full of shower
essentials completed the look, plus his flip-flops to
wear in the shower.

These flip-flops have another use, killing flies in
summer. They are amazing, one go whaaaap!!! under
Alex's deft hand.

I can (and do) live with all the rain, snow, ice and
wind. One of the scariest things was the gales we
had the winter before last! They ripped through the
campsite's forest at 100mph, bringing down branches
and trees, squashing caravans, sending awnings up
trees.

Our caravan was knocked, kicked, bumped with this
screaming sound like an enormous baby having a
tantrum. I thought it would just take off with us
inside it, no chance of getting out in NZ though!

Throughout the spring, summer and even into autumn,
people would come in their caravans, and tents.
Our view would go from fantastic to non-existent in
a couple of hours. Friday's were the worst. We would
wake up in the morning, go to work and upon our
return be totally surrounded by all sorts and sizes
of caravans, motor homes and tents. Some of the
motor homes were so big that they could only park
the other end of the site. Others had originally
been coaches and converted (we really like these).
Most people were very pleasant, quiet and courteous.

Leonie (who helped in the office) lived on the site.
But, if you got onto the wrong side of her, not many
people live to tell the tale!!

V V glad that we got on well.

On Sundays, we would have a lie in. After a cup of
tea, we'd get up, unzip the front of the awning
and have breakfast. That was about the time most
people started packing up and going home, or maybe
traveling to another part of the country. As the
caravans and campers trundled past our site, we
would start singing " another one bites the dust,
and another one's gone, another one's gone..." It
was great to get our view back!

Another one bites the dust...

"You're doing a great job!
Don't get drunk and lose it"
— Captain Jack

Good and bad things about Living on a Campsite:

1. You have no address. And, if you have no address, you didn't exist.

2. We didn't have to pay council tax, so that was the upside, even if you didn't exist.

3. We tried to get a postbox. Impossible! As we had to have an address.

4. That's why we wanted it you...........?????????

5. We weren't on the internet. We'd pick up emails, check on the Tunisian money status, and apply for jobs on the nightly visits to McDonalds car park.

6 If we were feeling flusher than we normally were, Alex would get an Muc D's ice-cream for 99p.

7 We had pay-as-you-go mobiles, and they were always running out of credit at the worst possible time, but better than a contract, not that we would have been given a contract anyway.

8 We often couldn't afford pre-pay vouchers, IOU £3 credit was always used, rather like the petrol gauge in Alex's car.

9 Food - spiceee and tasteeeee - get cooking! I'll have more recipes later on.

10 Pay your rent weekly if you can, so you don't have to hide from landlady.

11 Don't waste petrol. Walk if you can. If you can't, just turn the engine off in heavy traffic.

12 If you're lucky enough to have the odd drink, have red wine as it's v good for you, and essential to keep your spirits up.

Beauty a la Me

I use aqueous cream on my body. It's a couple of
quid and it comes in a huge tub. If we don't have
any, any, any money, I use it on my face in place of
simple. It's fine.

I use makeup wipes around my eyes, but instead of
using just one, as you are directed, I divide them
into sixteenths, same with cotton wool pads.

My makeup lasts and lasts and lasts. I brush on my
lipstick as its all disappeared into the base. I
still use make-up from a course I did which must be
about three years ago.

One afternoon, I had an interview for some extra
support work. I went into Debenhams, over to the
Chanel counter and sat perched on the make-up chair
while she did my entire face.

After wandering over to perfumes, I liberally
sprayed on Prada Candy before I left.

I felt great and exuded confidence.

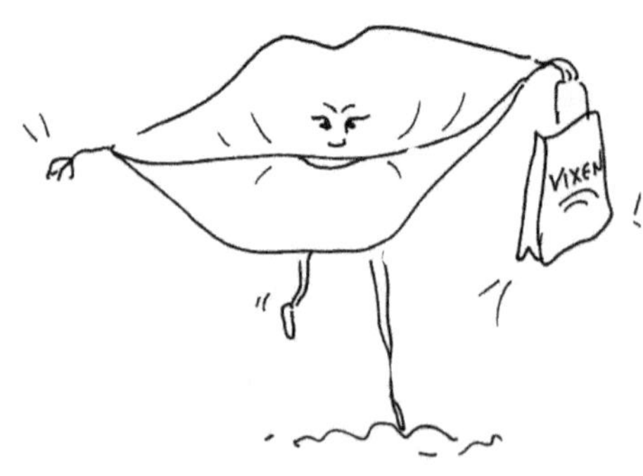

You're Not As Young As You Think

Yes, it's awful how age just creeps up on you.

You know your getting old by:

Gobsmacked 1
"He only looks about twelve and he's driving a car."
Or "He looks about fourteen and he's/she's a doctor/
lawyer/pilot?"

Gobsmacked 2
You're in the supermarket stocking up with food and
wine, comparing prices, and you're approached by a
serious looking, elderly person in front of a stand.
He asks you in a lowered tone, whether you have done
a will? What the…??
"Yes I have thank you, and you're not in it." Do
they have NO standards?

Gobsmacked 3
When you get up in the morning, and go to work
with sheet marks on your face. They do come out
eventually, I suppose it's just lack of collagen ;(
Or, you still see a sunglass mark either side of
your nose from yesterday.

Gobsmacked 4

Noses and ears get bigger and hairier.

Gobsmacked 5

You can't always control your farts. Mortifying!

Gobsmacked 6

You start to fantasise about shopping trolleys on wheels! Very handy, and a good way to mow down people in front of you.

" Beauty begins the moment you decide to be yourself"

— Coco Chanel

Morning Has Broken

First thing in the morning, we had a routine as only
one person could move around. If it was my turn,
I would get up and wash my face, put on the kettle,
put teabags in the cups, put cream on my face, add
hot water, put foundation on, take the tea bags out,
put milk in the tea.

Or, Alex would get up first, put the kettle on, put
teabags on his eyes, foundation on the mugs…

Oh, just kidding!!

But, after the night we spent camping, the caravan
was sheer luxury.

One morning we were up early as per usual, having
a cup of tea in bed and we saw lots of deer just
outside the caravan, feeding. It was very calm and
quite still.

* * * * * **M A G I C** * * * * *

"The earth has
music for those who listen"
— William Shakespeare

Chapter 4.

X-mas In London

We spent Christmas looking after Laura's flat
in Brixton. After living in the caravan it was
luxurious to have the space to move around and
different rooms to be in!

We tried not to think about last Christmas, which
we spent at our beach house in NZ, in the blazing
sun!
As we sat in Laura's front room with a glass of
wine, I started to remember…

Whooosh

    Whoooooosh!!!!!

       It's

          coming

            back   to

               me !!!!

"There were once two people in their latter years,
who moved all the way to New Zealand on a…"
"Yes, Daisy…"
"On a fishing boat…?"
"You could get there on a fishing boat, but they went
on a Plane. It took a very, very long time to get
there.

All day and all night…

big ears
little ears.

Moving To N'Z

We flew into Auckland and started looking for jobs.
Alex and I stayed at the Four Seasons Hotel which
was cheap and clean, only problem was, the lift
didn't always work and we stayed on the 14th floor.
Imagine that! Good for the thigh muscles I think.

I did have a nightmarish experience at that hotel. I
went to the loo in the middle of the night, shut the
door and didn't turn on the outside bathroom light.
I made my way to the loo, still half asleep. There
were no windows in the bathroom, I sleepily tried to
find the loo paper and couldn't. I was suddenly wide
awake, my panic rose?!! I stood up and groped my
way around, turning on the shower by mistake which
went all over my head, grabbing towels blindly which
fell at my feet, bottles falling to the floor. I was
in tears by now and I might suffocate in the loo?
Imagine the write-up in the papers, "Bathroom You'd
Die For!!" HELP!' I cried knocking on the walls. I
could hear Alex's deep snores. Suddenly, I didn't
care who heard me, I started knocking harder, then
HARDER and eventually THUMPING ON THE WALL WITH BOTH
FISTs…

At last he woke up, and
thought...?? He came to the loo
door, opened it, and I burst out.

Alex had an interview right up in the far north
of New Zealand, a stunning four hour drive from
Auckland. That was in his first week. Oh Yes! Seemed
like fate. We hired a car and decided to stay the
night at a motel in Kaitaia. He interviewed the next
day and spent ages being shown around. A good sign
we thought.

Before returning to Auckland we drove around the
peninsular. It was beautiful and right up at the
very tip of NZ, Pacific Sea on one side, Tasman Ocean
on the other. Bare white beaches, blue, blue seas
and sky and not very many people. Ideal.

We didn't hear anything about the job for weeks.
Alex phoned numerous times and was told that it was
all good, they merely hadn't confirmed it. Annoying!

We applied to NZ House sitters which was an online
sitting service. You would go into a place for
anything from 2 weeks to one year. It was great. You
might feed dogs/cats/hens/birds/lamas etc. We got
immediate success rate and were turning houses down.

kiwi house sitter details.
Sitter 1 : Alex
Sitter 2 : kate
Preferred Location : All NZ

We are currently sitting until
the 16 th July. We are a couple in
our 50's (Just 50 in my case !)
who enjoy walking, animals,
country life but city's too.
Your pets will be very well looked
after. I grew up on a farm and
have had loads of pets. Alex
has had horses, cat and goldfishes
My mother's two dogs adore him
We have references, PR and
police checks, and are both honest
and trustworthy.
Looking forward to hearing from
you.
Witt

A cheesy photograph which I won't
include!

A few weeks later I was waiting for Alex on K.
Rd, which is filled with sex shops, transvestites,
prostitutes and uber cool companies. He hugged me and
said that he had just received a phone call, he HAD
got the job in Kaitaia confirmed. **Fantastic!!**

I had some freelance advertising work in Auckland
and thought I'd be able to find support work
anywhere, as people always need support/care in some
form?

We speedily moved up to Kaitaia and came across a
small cove called Rangiputa. We loved it and wanted
to live in/near it. There were wooden houses in
all sorts of colours set amongst Pohutukawas which
have beautiful red flowers at Christmas. The houses
climbed up the hill facing the expanse of sea, with
a white strip of sand in the distance, between yet
more trees.

An English couple ran the one and only motel and
they gave us the number of a woman who owned a place
on Tokerau beach. We did a drive by and it turned
out to be a large and new-ish bungalow, opposite the
beach with most of the front made of glass.
We thought it was way out of our price range.
It wasn't.

We moved in for a few days over Christmas, but
Sandra (landlady) had already arranged for the
bungalow to be let for a week over the New Year.
We moved back to Rangiputa and spent the next five
days at a house with the most incredible sea views!
It was like being on the top deck of a ship, looking
out to sea with a whisper of land in the distance.

But,

the house had

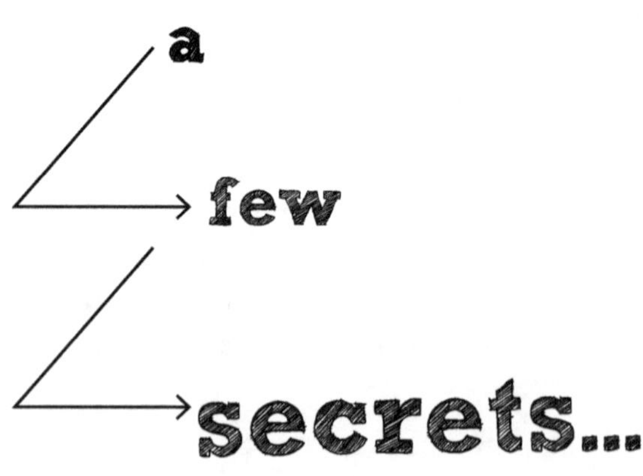

When you opened the door you were enveloped in a
foul, rotting smell. It seemed as if the house had
been suddenly deserted. There were clothes left all
over the place, beds unmade, photos displayed, soap
and cosmetics in the bathroom. Very weird.

We looked at each other and thought something bad
has happened here!

There was a mezzanine floor which was a double
bedroom with sliding doors onto the deck. We went
downstairs and opened the sliding doors to another
deck. Alex cleaned the kitchen thoroughly and all
around the living area. It helped a bit but the rot
was still there.

He suddenly rushed to the loo.

I could have put on Motorhead very loudly, or put my
fingers in my ears and danced a crazy jig...

I heard all the sounds of diarrhoea...!!!

On the first night we got badly bitten by mosquitoes.
The next day, I looked everywhere for a mosquito
net which I found stuffed under the bed. It provided
an extra obstacle course for Alex, who was still
spending the majority of his time in the loo!

The diarrhoea lasted three long days, he was well
pooped by the end, pardon the pun.

E
M
A
HE
A

With two deck windows permanently open lots of
swallows would swoop into the kitchen/lounge circle
and then leave out of the mezzanine floor/our
bedroom. I think they had a nest under the deck. Two
of the younger chicks flew in and got stuck inside.
Alex had to very carefully rescue them, with my
helpful instructions;) If I wasn't human, I'd hope
to be a swallow or a dolphin. I reckon Alex would be
a deer/gazelle.

We found out more about what happened to the family.
I gather that she had suddenly left with their two
children and there was another lover involved.

He disappeared to Australia.

We did think that the wife and children might have
been under the floorboards but thats another story!

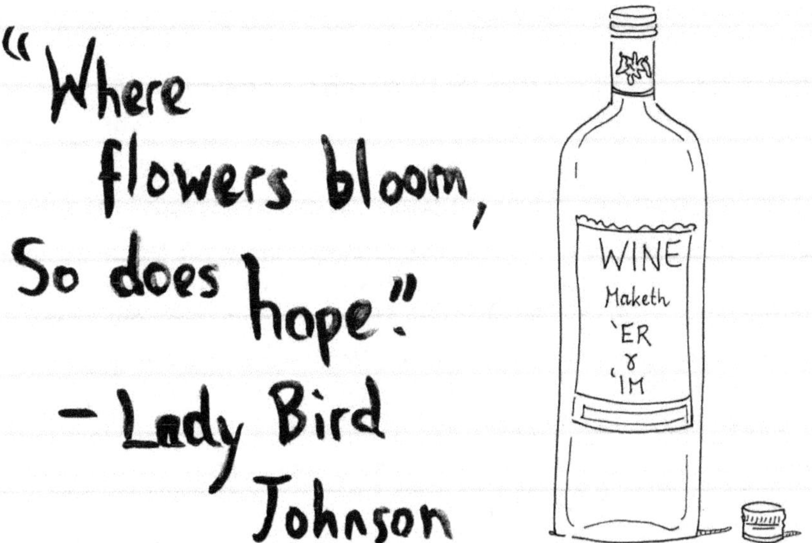

Life On the Beach

In the new year we moved into our bungalow opposite
the beach. We had a fantastic time, sometimes making
love on the front deck, hearing the waves crashing
on the beach and Split Ends/Marian Faithful playing
in the background. It was the height of summer, when
Alex came home from work we would pull back the huge
glass doors and sit on the front patio with a glass
of New Zealand Sauvignon Blanc, glasses chilled in
the freezer. We discovered a local Sauvignon Blanc
called "Fat Bird", what a good name - had to try
it! We went for walks along the white sandy beach
holding hands and loving life. Neither of us missing
hordes of people.

There was one garage with a small shop attached and
a fish and chip shop where you could take fish you'd
caught. That was about it.

Kaitaia's a very small town. I joined a Maori
support group who were a lively and beautiful group
of people. When I went in, they would rub noses
which is the Maori hello and welcome. Er, I think
that's what they said ?)

Everything moved at a much slower pace than I was
used to and seemed to take a longer time to be
accepted and get work.

Alex had a very, very ancient company truck which
according to Ralph (his boss) was going to be
upgraded into a flashier 4 Wheel Drive. You had to
put shopping bags over the front seats and on the
floor before you got in, otherwise all sorts of black
oil and dirt would get everywhere. Top speed was a
rattling and rolling 40 kph, uphill 25 kph, if you
were lucky. It was also missing one gear. But when
Alex drove it to work, he was in paradise!! His
words.

Beaut-y-ful?

When I first returned to the UK, I wanted to do
something else, something practical and a complete
change from advertising (being out-skilled as I was/
am).

I applied for a course in holistic therapy but
it was cancelled due to lack of interest. So I
did beauty therapy, level 1. Big mistake! When
I realised I wasn't going to be that great as a
beautician, I thought Hang on, someone must need
my skills somewhere? Maybe I could concentrate on
people who are going through a generaly shitty time
such as cancer, nervous breakdowns etc. Where better
than at hospital! I could do beauty therapy on the
patients admitted. I was filled with new enthusiasm!

Would they be looking at my beauty treatment skills
or want someone to talk to? I hoped the latter.
Still, I'm not sure I would have liked me as a
Beauty Therapist, especially if there was hot wax
involved.

It's not easy to have wax at the right temperature.
Too hot will burn and might very well take half your
leg off. And too cold makes a sticky mess.
But, it does get 10/10 for taking a patient's mind
off all operations/treatments.

Alex let me practice on him. He's had legs waxed,
back waxed, facial massage, manicures, I drew
the line at a pedicure. Make-up on, make-up off,
eyelashes permed, eyebrows dyed.

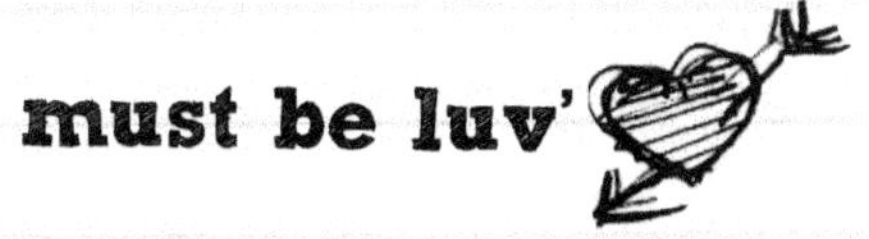

I saw an ad in the NZ local paper, "Looking For A Beauty Therapist in Keri Keri". I was desperate to get something, so thought I should apply!

It was a long and mountainous drive to get there and mobile coverage was nil.

I'd arranged to meet up with the owner, Sian. A flat white coffee and a large slice of carrot cake later, I'd agreed to everything. She was mid-thirties, and chattering away like I was the prodigal daughter that would save her company.

Hmmm, I was beginning to feel more and more uneasy!

But, they were desperate for staff, which I thought was a good sign?

After going there for two days with a few new recruits, we were told to practice our facial massage skills on each other. It suddenly reminded me of beauty college, I thought no, this isn't for me. I can bluff in person but not in practise.

Anyway it was:
a. Too far to travel
b. Sian was a real nut
c. Not a cooky nut, but more of a nutter nut
d. And I was a crap beautician

Keri Keri had a lucky escape.

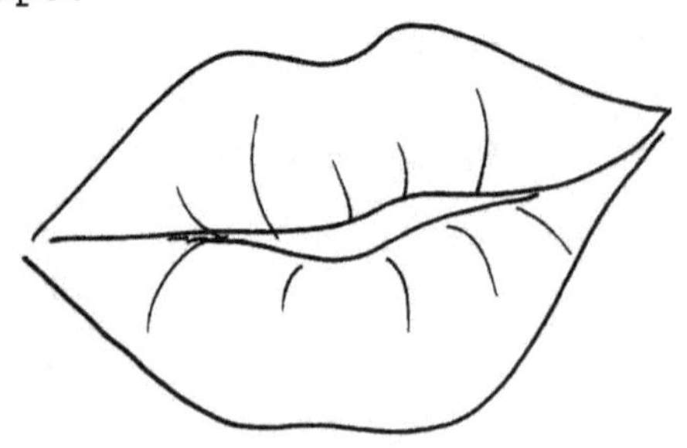

Rain, Rain, Go to Spain, Never Show Your Face Again

Sometimes I would get a lift with Alex into Kaitaia.
The journey was about twenty miles along the
beautiful peninsular.

I used to kill the day looking for jobs in the
paper, checking in at three support agencies and
treating myself to one amazing flat white coffee.
Everyone was really nice, full of good advice but
still no job.

I was walking up to Pack n' Save which is the hugest
supermarket with a great selection of food, when the
sky turned dark, and the heavens opened.

I could almost see a weather god right above me,
rumbling with laughter, massive hose in hand with an
endless supply of water straight over MY head. Not
that I'm paranoid or anything.

I swear I got soaked. I had to take off my shoes as
they were full of water, clothes, carrier bags,
my hair was soaked, mascara ran down my face as I
stooped blindly along. Water is incredibly heavy!! I
felt like falling to my knees and howling. I didn't
care any more, I had tried to get a effing job and
had even applied for a job in sodding Pack n'Save
where I was sodding heading...
nothing,

Nothing!!!

It was suddenly a tropical downpour.

A car stopped, a woman leant across and opened
the door, she offered me a lift. Was this an
angel? If so, she had a nice, new, white BMW. I
suddenly felt more cheerful.

'Look at me, I'm drenched..!!' stating the
obvious, mascara running down my cheeks like
tears, teeth chattering, 'But, thanks a lot
anyway..!!!' I turned and started walking away.
"c'mon, get in…" she said
with an aussie accent, giving me a pile of
towels to sit on. There was a black Labradoodle
sitting on the back seat peering quizzically at
me … "Oh mon dieu elle a l'air a moitie noyee.."
She has bare feet…? Must be of kiwi descent! A
very strange one indeed!!

Still, she might play catch with me…'

I suddenly envied the dog. It would be nice to be a dog in a loving home. You'd be free to sleep whenever you want, play all day or even run off knowing that your owner would run behind you shouting your name, again and again, as you bounded into the trees and hid.

Other people would make decisions for you, there would be no work, no trying to fit in, you would even have a human to pick up your poo and pop the contents in a poo bin. Makes you wonder, who is who's pet?

I got in gratefully.

After that horrible soaking experience, Alex bid and bought a car on Trade Me. We spent more than we had budgeted for. Alex and I took the coach down to Auckland, paid for the car and drove it back.

It was a black Isuzu Mu with a fantastic sound system, giant subwoofer between the two front seats.

Oh Yeah!! * * * * *

* * * * * It soon became Disaster No:1 ....

I applied for a job working with young people as a negotiator between parent and child. It was a council run position and came into ch 2. I spent ages on the form, writing and re-writing it again and again before sending it off. I didn't hear anything at all about this position but knew this would take ages as the council have to check you out. Not necessarily a good thing in my case! The job was in Whangaparoa, a lovely place on the coast.

Unfortunately, (there's quite a few
'unfortunately's' in this book) Alex's boss was
a pratt. He was from Auckland and people from
there had a reputation as JAFA, which means,
Just Another Fucking Aucklander.

(Er, hold on, I lived in Auckland too…)

Alex was forced to resign from his job.

I can't tell you how that affected us, our bubble
had well and truly exploded.

We had no Plan B.

Alex and I silently packed up and left in the
very early morning, not daring to look around at
what we were leaving behind.

Our paradise.

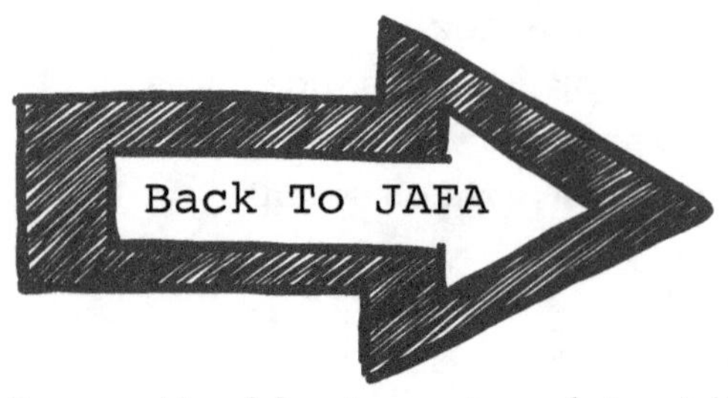

I wasn't able to get a job while in Kataia, but sod's law, my phone rang twice in the car when we were half way to Auckland. One call was from Te Hiku (Maori place) offering me support work at long last and the other was from Okaru Estate, Kaitiai, offering me a job.

What?? **? ?**

But it was too late.

I was completely and utterly broke by this time, my credit card was maxed out which I discovered at the Warehouse, the cheapest store in NZ.

I was trying to buy six packets of chocolate éclairs made by Werthers.

I handed over my credit card and waited … It bounced up to the ceiling and came crashing down like a big fist!

You can't have any Chocolate éclairs made by Werthers, so there!

... I crept out :(

Meanwhile, back in Brixton, I woke with a jump as the clock struck midnight. We were still in Laura's flat at Christmas time. I glanced over to Alex who was asleep, or maybe like me, deep in thought. I finished my wine and stretched, Laura would be back tomorrow.

And we'd return to the caravan site.

"I see no ships, just hardships"

— Captain Jack

Chapter 5

Back to reality……

We drove up the grit road to the campsite and looked over at our caravan. At least it was still upright which was a relief, though the awning had come down in the gales.

We owed two month's rent to the campsite plus the ongoing rent. Our priority was: Petrol x 2, Food and Rent. It was nice of Laura to lend us her flat and to get away from all these pressures. The manager lived on the site. I avoided her. She knew that we didn't have a towing vehicle but we couldn't lose the caravan as well. Our home.

There was a nice outgoing woman who worked in the office, she became the go between as we were trying to get up to date with our rent. I became friendly with her when Alex just seemed to disappear off the face of the earth. Well, that's what I thought anyway.

I texted him three times. Where was he? He always texted me back. I had very little money on my pay-as-you-go mobile but was worried and called him. Nothing!! This is what I thought. "Serious car crash/pile up on the M27. Ten ambulances rush to the scene. It's carnage, bodies everywhere, one car over the other side. Alex is unconscious, in an ambulance, the phone was ringing in the fire engulfed car but no-one could get to it. Fire engines arrive, water everywhere. He has a heart attack/stroke in the ambulance. Paramedic administers CPR. Not looking good. There was no connection to me in his wallet or to the campsite where we lived. How would they know? How would I know?"

I went over to the office, off-loaded all this to the nice-outgoing woman in the office, was almost wringing my hands. She looked out of the office window, 'Isn't that Alex…?' He waved, just like the lone ranger riding into town amid a cloud of dust. I suddenly felt angry!

Alex said he had written me a text but because he had no money left on his pay-as-you-go, I didn't get it. He'd just been to see John, his old boss at Fastcrete. There might be some work there, pending quite a number of things! I forgave him.

Alex! Get Back To Work;)

Alex has a friend called Fred, in fact his ex-brother in law. He has a company called Fred's Lubricants (sounds a bit rude) which blends, decants, packages, sells and delivers lubricant oils. Alex was able to work for him running the office while he and Clio (his partner) went off on a biking holiday. Alex started working a couple of weeks before Fred was going, which was great as he didn't have any work.

Fred, Julian and Alex

Alex, Fred and Julian go way back. They would spend two weeks in the summer riding motorcycles on their Annual European Tour.

They kept to "A" roads, taking in scenery, hairpin bends and camped in random places.

France, Andora, Swiss Alps, Italy, Spain, Croatia
are places they visited. Fred had some t-shirts
printed on the Croatian trip. On the front they
all said, "European Tour 08, Croatia or Bust." On
the back Fred had: "Big Boss. If You're Not The
Leader The View Never Changes." Alex had: "Keep Your
Distance, Tendency To Fall Off." Julian had: "If You
See Me On My Own, I'm Lost."

Julian used to overtake Fred at the wrong time, just
when Fred and Alex were going to turn left.

On one tour, Fred was on his Harley when his exhaust
pipe started to leak and needed welding. They went
to a garage near the campsite. The owner said he had
a welding set and would let them use it but couldn't
find his welding mask! Alex (who's a mechanic)
thought, "what the hell" and made a mask out of
Fred's, Julian's and his sunglasses and then welded
up the hole.

How's that for:
"Up there for thinking,
down there for dancing,"
can do, attitude!
— Captain Jack

Alex Has More Work With Fred

When Fred came back off holiday he asked Alex to
stay on, as he needed to spend some time seeing
customers, sorting out new suppliers and a few other
things.

On Monday morning, Alex was stuck in heavy traffic,
he texted Fred that he was running late. Fred
texted straight back saying he was in hospital with
two broken ribs, punctured lung, damage to his
foot, hands and various bruises. He was out on his
motorbike (I should say he owns a 2.3cc Triumph
Rocket 3) and as he was overtaking a line of cars a
white van pulled out alongside him. He had nowhere
to go but straight on to the verge on the other side
of the road. He nearly got back onto the road, but
a branch caught his right arm, he and his bike were
sliding along the road. Luckily, a Doctor was at the
scene, able to administer first aid and wait for the
ambulance.

Alex was able to stay on a good few months while
Fred was recuperating.

Back to Fastcrete?

Alex dropped in to his old company in Salisbury, he hadn't heard anything from them re: work. I admired him for going back in. He was looking for any work like driving, packing, anything! They said they might have some driving work but none materialised.

A few months later they were toying around with starting up a new branch in the Midlands, and they called Alex in and said,

"WOULD HE BE INTERESTED IN RUNNING IT??"

What?

We were told to spend the night up there and see if we wanted to move.

So that's what Alex and I did.

It was beautiful farmland around the cities. I suppose being an ignorant southerner I was expecting a cliché of built up industrial towns with lots of closed factories and people speaking with funny accents;)

Some of it is very like that (and I'm not talking about people with a funny accents) with boarded up buildings in certain areas and disused factories. But on a work level you're in the region of Birmingham, Wolverhampton, Liverpool,Manchester, Leeds.

We drove around some very pretty villages.

We loved it! Luckily.

It was a good move for Alex, he deserved some luck
and great that he would be working in the same
company again. I wasn't so sure about me but felt ok
to give it a go, jo.

But the whole move and finding a suitable warehouse
took ages, and ages, and ages! We were just starting
to think it's never going to happen.

Alex was still filling in for Fred, otherwise there
was no financial way that we would have kept going.

But then they bought a warehouse in: Stafford.

Stafford?? Where's that!

I kept getting it confused with Sheffield.

We paid off the campsite rent, well, Alex did, plus
the current rent. Which meant that we were even more
broke than before if that's possible.

Impossible!

Working at Fred's helped a lot as he got on very
well with both him and his brother. Alex was
starting to put on weight which was nice to see and
to get his confidence back.

I found the whole thing hard, frequent conversations
with Laura kept me sane. I discovered that I havn't
lost my sense of humour, it's even blacker than it
was!! I still had the embarrassment of resigning
from my job. A job which I'd asked for and one where
I had just accepted a permanent role. What would I
say?

Then I thought about a transfer to Stafford with the
same company. I would be able to start work right
away. Alex had been given a company van so we could
tow the caravan up. All good thought I. Did my last
naggy email chasing up Tunisian money from Muc D's
carpark.

ME: Any news yet? It's been almost two years?

REPLY: …No,no money yet. It's in the Tunisian
courts!!!

ME: I know I've asked you before but is there any
chance of an advance…? I've got all these moving
expenses coming up.

REPLY: I'm sorry, but we can't give you an advance…

As they say in advertising, 'back to the drawing
board'. No Money for Muc D's Ice Cream - 99p.

Up, Down, Up, Down.

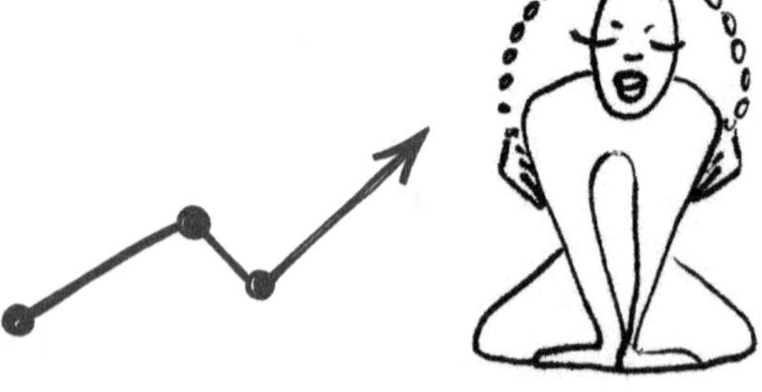

<u>Stafford/Sheffield?</u>

Alex set off for Stafford in his van pulling the
caravan.

Me, following behind in my trusty, lusty, super
star car.

With two v v worn tyres! Oh well, what the hell!!
When your no's up it's up that's all! Alex would get
a moving allowance for the first three months. We
thought to ourselves we might!!!!???? be on an
upward slope but still had a long way to go.

I was glad to move to a neutral place. One minute we
would be getting along well, next, things would take
a downward turn. Again.

"If you try, you risk failure. If you don't, you ensure it"

— Source unknown

Chapter 6.

<u>Yeehaaaar!! Stafford Rocks</u>.

Alex unlocked the gates and we stood side by side, looking at our vast, new, luxurious home. Oh ok, it wasn't that luxurious but somewhere we could park the caravan for a few months of not paying any rent.

Sigh!!

The work would start the very next day, converting this huge space into an office + warehouse. It was amazing seeing it all take place around you. Literally.

The caravan was parked to one side of the warehouse, with two chairs and a table in front of it. Unfortunately we couldn't put up the awning, it would have given us a bit more privacy. Alex would be up at 7.15am and making some tea. He would step outside the caravan pulling on his thick reflective yellow jacket (I love that jacket, it's so Diesel) jeans and work boots. He raised the warehouse's huge corrugated door and drove my car which was parked in front of the caravan, out to the front yard.

Fastcrete was now open. It was a hive of activity during the day. Up went the breeze-block partitions for the showroom, and office. Down went the mezzanine floor and stairs. We had chippies, builders, plumbers, electricians etc. and that was just inside. Outside there were ten men fully concreting the yard. Alex painted, swept up, put the ceiling lights in etc. He project managed the whole thing with visits from Fastcrete, bringing different skills.

103

They all arrived at 7.45 am. Can you imagine all the
dust and grime we've breathed in!!

But although we were saving on campsite rent which
was a good thing, we were still completely broke.

I'd met Alex's boss a few times, he was supremely fit
for someone of his age.

Nipping down drain holes, driving forklifts at top
speed, racing cars, knocking out walls with his
bare fists. OK, that last one might be a little far
fetched! He hated wasting money and would rather do
it himself than get someone else to do it.

Right now it's Saturday 10.45pm, Alex is painting
the new office ceiling wearing black over-all's and a
peaked hat, which is fast becoming white. Fastcrete
leads by example.

After we moved into the warehouse the caravan had
some r&r and tlc. We gave it a really good clean
outside, it was quite filthy especially on the roof
which was underneath trees. We slowly moved our stuff
out, feeling a little guilty and stored it at the
new works.

About the same time the fridge packed up. Alex
stripped it out and found that it was only the
switch that had broken. He repaired/cleaned the
caravan.

As chance would have it the hot water system packed up too. This meant no hot showers or even cold ones. It was now January and bloody cold and wet. Where could we have a shower? We thought gym's? Too expensive. Swimming pools? Too expensive.

Then Alex suddenly said, "They have showers at the motorway services…" I said, "brilliant!" So we gathered up all our shower stuff and went along to have a look. About twenty-five minutes later on the M6 we came to our closest service station. They did indeed have showers and, better still, we were able to get the internet too.

Plus it was warm. Plus, it was free.

So that's where we went for our weekly shower (Don't you think people these days are way too clean!!!!!)

All went well for the first few Sunday's. Well, it's Gods day of rest so that had to be a good thing.

I have long hair, but would rather have a bottle of wine than pay to have it cut. I put it up so it's out of my face and lucky me, despite my advancing years my hair's dark brown, but with increasing streaks of silver.

This is the most natural colour I've had in my entire life. Alex has a number 2 so he's ok.

This particular Sunday was very different. I went first as usual, Alex began to wonder if everything was ok!! I was taking an incredible amount of time.

When I finally came back and explained that when I was washing my hair the drain became blocked the water level had risen, spilling out over the floor which made everything on the floor float or sink including my trainers, socks, jeans… served me right for putting them on the floor like some teenager!

And, annoyingly, the hot water supply would simply go off after one minute, so you had to keep on pressing the button. If you didn't get a chance to press the button while washing and shampooing your hair, it would suddenly become freezing again. I wish I had extra arms like that Indian God. It wouldn't have been a problem then though I might look like a spider.

On top of this I heard the cleaner armed with a mop, ttuutt…tuuuttt…ing noises, banging her mop against the door, trying to clear up all the water that was flooding under, while cursing in Polish. I don't blame her, I'm her worst nightmare.

I thought grumpily that Alex's shower always went off without a hitch. We decided next time we'd try our luck in the services on the opposite side as we weren't sure I'd be allowed in again.

Next Sunday we set off in his company truck, but half way there realised we'd forgotten to bring the rucksack with all of our washing stuff. To hell with it!

We looked for a launderette, at least the clothes would be clean.

Something strange happened to my sweatshirt while in the drier. It appeared burnt. I blamed the tumble dryer until upon closer investigation, two teabags fell out of the pocket. Oh, shit! My fault. Another job for Vanish.

We returned once again to 'camp'. Alex put up a washing line as per usual, tied between the handle on the front of the caravan and the trolley jack, to dry all the things that were 'delicates.' He wheeled out the E-Space heater. Ignited, it was like a jet engine, noisy and almost as big that burnt diesel.

If you shut your eyes with the click of the overhead lockers, it was like being on a plane, going somewhere, anywhere, hot!

Alex had to go down to Salisbury, Fastcrete's
head office. He had the latest, updated photos of
the building work inside the Stafford Branch. What
excitement!

He showed photos to John, who was duly impressed
and then (unfortunately) borrowed the camera to
show Phil, his son who worked there too. He came
across some he hadn't seen, namely, Alex drying
his knickers in front of the e-space, waving at me
and pulling a silly face. Then he saw some more,
of the washing line with lots of clothes pegged
on and a general mess of sheets (clean luckily),
duvet covers, pillow cases over tables. I suppose
it must have looked like a gypsy camp, plus all of
the building things lying around. All heated by the
e-space. Not really his idea of the brand new depot!

John didn't say anything.

He didn't have to. But, he didn't
give us any more diesel.

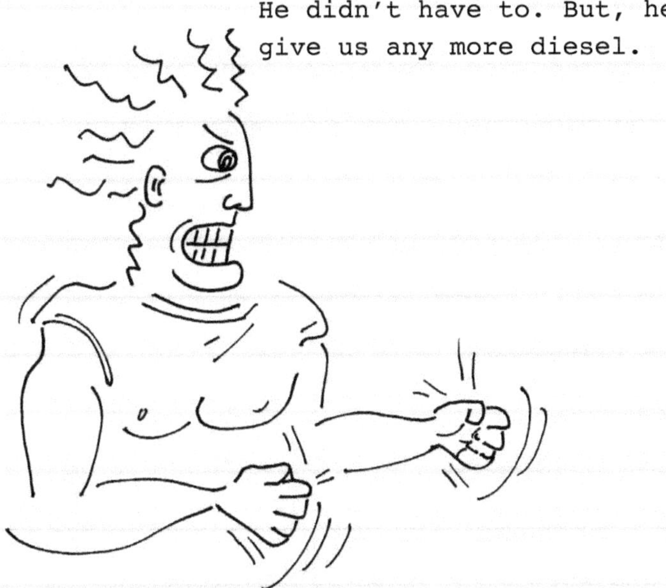

I got a transfer to Stafford from Salisbury as a support worker in one of their houses. I was able to start work right away, but would have a wait a month before I got paid! Oh, shit!!

The first evening, I was working as a 'shadow' with two other support workers. They asked me where I lived, and I answered in a caravan at Alex's windowless depot, which, I joked, was like a building site.

Joked?? Yes, it really was a building site.

They were completely speechless. Jenny lived with her boyfriend who was paralysed from the waist down. I thought, poor guy!! He was only young, about 18 or something. I asked how he did it? Apparently, he and a friend were casing the joint, he was on the roof and fell through. Ahmmm, some justice perhaps!!

"Do you have a telly?" Jenny asked hopefully.
"No…" I said.
Her face fell.
"But, what you do??"
"Oh, we like cooking and reading … sometimes watch a DVD…"
Then I added, "Do you know anywhere that has public showers? At the moment we use the motorway services…"

She looked horrified.

In the meantime, Alex and I had visited a few campsites and discovered that you were unable to live on a campsite all year. In actual fact, you had to move on after 28 days! Most of them didn't have facilities and were also closed in winter.

What shall we do??

I had fears of having to camp in a field full of
cows, pigs and/or an aggressive bull. Can you
imagine, mud everywhere our awning full of sheep.
All I needed was a baby and we'd be a living
nativity scene.

Where would we get water? Empty the loo, have a
shower, empty the wastewater??
Once again I heard the survival bubble pop.

I felt sick.

We had moved up here, I had left my support job in
Salisbury, things between Alex and I weren't always
that great. It's the things you don't say to each
over as well as the things you do.

I talked to Jenny again, she suggested a trip to
Stafford and Rural as we were effectively homeless!

She was completely right, we were homeless!

We couldn't live at Fastcrete's new depot that much longer and we couldn't save up a deposit, rent in advance etc. of a private house/flat.

We went to Stafford and Rural, filled out a form plus two references from previous landlords which Alex luckily had, plus a character reference from work. They were very helpful and advised us to go and see the council and apply there as well.

I never usually use my health, which is very good as it happens.

Fifteen years ago I had a tumour in my heart, which went undiagnosed for about three years. I had a heart attack and a stroke before they found it and surgery the next day when they did.

Survival prognosis = 30%.

I went to the council the next day, took my pills with me and said that so far my health was fine but I was afraid with all the dust, paint and so on that I/we were breathing in would affect my/our health. It was like living on an enclosed building site with our caravan at the centre.

I honestly thought they wouldn't give us anything at all. Same old treatment! We had very little money and were a hopeless case. At times like that I thoroughly hate myself! I know Alex does too.

The council guy made the right noises but I still
left feeling nothing will happen. Frankly, it
doesn't seem to where I'm concerned.

He called me the next day, he had a flat which had
become vacant with Sanctuary housing. The rent was
affordable, with a concierge at night, entry phones
and barrier to the car park.

I was completely speechless.

I went to see it and thought it could be really
nice, especially the huge window in the lounge.
But I was still distrustful! We had to supply bank
statements, I thought here we go, living on my
overdraft as I was.

Alex looked better on paper, but not much.

We left it with them and then a few days later, had
to go to Sanctuary's head-office in Stoke.

We had to pay a weeks rent in advance, that was
it!!! And, we could move in right away. Amazing!!!!

We were supplied with a pantone chart and able to
paint the flat whatever color we wanted.
Wow!! Dulux would deliver it the next day and it was
free.

The kitchen had new worktops and cupboards and the
bathroom had been professionally painted with a new
loo.

We had to buy a fridge, cooker and we needed to put
a carpet/flooring down.

So, we set to work.

Alex painted all the walls. I painted the bathroom
pipes and skirting boards. Choosing the colour's was
largely left to me. I chose a burnt yellow for the
lounge, oyster for the hall and bedrooms, grey for
the kitchen and white for the bathroom. We didn't
have a fridge, so milk and eggs had to placed next
to the window so they wouldn't go off. We didn't have
a cooker, so we were eating cold food or cooking in
the caravan first before coming 'home.'

It was great to have a home. We could fit two and a
bit of our caravan into the lounge. Our expenses
were much less, as Alex didn't have to pay petrol.
I could go to work and back on one tank of petrol
per month! It would have been three
times a week in Salisbury.

Alex had a relocation allowance,
when he got paid we bought a
fridge/freezer from the Hospice for
£60.00. The Hospice is next door to
Alex's new depot. It was an amazing
warehouse that sold pretty much
anything, all second hand. I'm very
good at spotting bargains. In fact,
I like doing that. We bought a five
person cream settee, like new, for
£15. £15!!!!!! I thought it's got to
be a typo, probably should be £50.
It wasn't.

We tried to get it into the lift, but there was no
way it would fit. We tried to get it up the stairs
but it wouldn't fit through the fire doors. We tried
chopping it in half but couldn't put it back together
again. Oops ! It reminded me of when I was little.
I had two plaits, I chopped off the right plait and
chopped off the left plait, and then was surprised
that my new haircut was all un-even at the bottom.

We bought some kitchen and bathroom floor tiles
incredibly cheaply. Alex put those down. We bought
some pictures for £1 each to go on the wall. We got
our bed back, the dining table, chairs, coffee table.

We got pans, crockery, cutlery. Alex had some
hardboard at work, he put it down on the floors. That
looked a lot better.

We were starting to get our life back!

and

then

i

GOT

PAID

from 

TUNISIAAAAAAAAAAAA

!!!!!!!!!!!!!!!!!!!

!!!!!!!!!!!!!

!!!!

Chapter 7.

The light at the end of the tunnel

Could it really be the end of our story??

We have certainly had some good luck:

1)   Fastcrete and the move to Stafford!

2)   Getting paid from Tunisia at long last!!!

3)   The flat.

4)   The hospice.

5)   Our job's.

Alex and I have learnt a very valuable lesson with everything we've endured after returning from NZ.

We definitely would have done the same thing again!

BUT:

We wouldn't have bought the car.

We would have stayed in Auckland, or gone to Christchurch where they are rebuilding the City after the earthquake.

We wasted lots of money on hotels.

We wasted lots of money on Food/Drink.

* * * * * * * * * * * * *

Follow your dream,

But always have a Plan B!

Chasing the Pig

Six months later and our lounge is full of pictures
of all sorts. Some are originals or prints that are
really nice, bought once again from the hospice.

It's worth going in there often as they have stock
that comes and goes almost immediately. It's a
collecting ground for antique dealers.

I grabbed a couple of Egon Shiele prints that I've
always liked for £2.00.

Then I saw the pig.

He was in a field with a perfect almost human face
lovingly painted. There was a wooden shed to the
right of the picture which stood next to a few
strands of hay, all done in oils. The overall effect
was rich and warm, almost like burnished gold.

I leaned over and picked up the pig in great
excitement. I was sure it was a work of art for a
modest £2.00. I found the painters name written in
the left hand corner, W.H.Davis.

I looked him up on my trusty (old) Mac, which has
been with me for the last seven years without even a
service.

Yes, W.H.Davis was a sporting painter born 1783-1865.
His work featured cows, bulls, horses, pigs and dogs
all in stunning landscapes.
In fact he was appointed an animal painter to Queen
Victoria in 1839 and to William IV in 1847.

What???

I texted Alex with great excitement. We decided to email one of the main auction houses, attaching a photo of my find. I got a reply straight away!!

"I KNOW PEOPLE WHO WOULD ADORE THAT PIG!!!!"
Crazy, crazy, excitement by this stage.
It can't be. No. Yes. Maybe?

We were told to measure the canvas' height and width. We did everything he asked for and answered questions about this find. It was an unknown picture.

The auction house was in constant touch for a week or so.

Alex and I had already moved to Portugal, bought a house there on the cliffs over looking the sea near a beautiful village.

We had spent the money on food, wine, sarongs and nautical gear for our 60ft speed boat. Toyed with a swimming pool?? And cars, bikes.

I was just pulling in to Tesco when he called me.

I breathlessly answered,

" Yes "...

"It's a fake!"

Epilogue

So this is us two years on. We're still living in
the flat in Stafford and its grown around us into the
best of all flats. It's perfect at night through our
huge window where we see stars against an inky black
sky. You could be almost anywhere looking out over
anything your heart desires.

We're surrounded by furniture from the hospice, I
like not knowing it's history even though everything
here has one.

Work is going great for Alex. He's been asked to
get a quote to enlarge the Stafford office, workshop/
showroom. In our spare time, not that we have much,
we've started an online shop called Propernice,
selling Clothes for Her.

It gets better! We are now making clothes to sell.
That's the idea anyway and it's REALLY easy to make
clothes. Not. Alex is better at it as he's more
patient. It seems much more about the prep beforehand
and then the sewing is quite easy. Hmmm!

That's what we found out when we took some lessons
after having a few abortive goes. Why is everything
so friggin hard? Anyway, my mother bought us an
overlocker which is great! You sew along with
multiple needles and it chops off extra material
leaving a very neat edge. The trouble is the garment
gets smaller and smaller if i do it!

I'm still working my butt off at the same place. I
like it there, it has a sort of madness about it.
I've left twice but always come back for more. They
can't keep staff which is great for me as I'm on a 0hr
contract so pick up shifts in the week and not at the
weekends!

On a more cheerful note I received two tax rebates.
The first paid off my credit card !!! three cheers !!!
the second one bought a Jeep, Very Luxurious compared
to my Vitara. It's diesel, black and growls along
like a panther.

Laura, Alex and I have just got back from the South
Island of NZ where we went for my sons wedding in
Queenstown. We had a great time, lots of laughter and
Alex and I buried a few ghosts.

We will return even if it's the last thing we do!

Other recipes from men'u
Feta Spaghetti

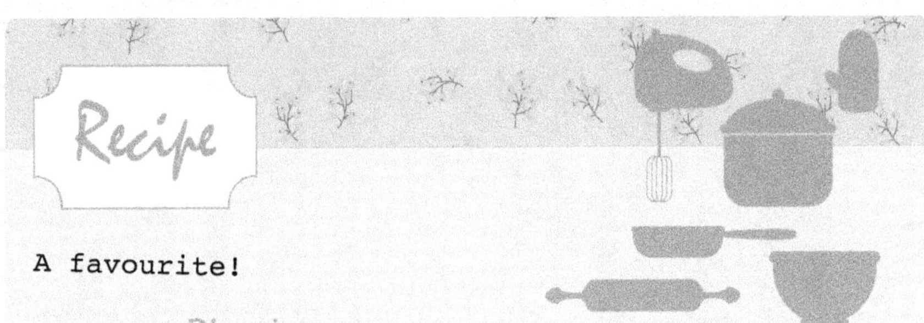

A favourite!

Directions

You'll need: Mortar & pestle or some way of crushing the almonds plus two hungry people.

Do the almonds first, that way they are done. Grate the Parmesan cheese. Break up the feta into small squares.

You'll need a frying pan and a saucepan for the spaghetti.

Take the frying pan, heat up some olive oil, when it's hot add the onion and garlic. When that is starting to brown, add the leek. In the meantime you're stirring it like a mad woman. Next add the mushrooms, when starting to brown, add a splash of dark soy sauce, and the peppers.

In the meantime, I find boiling the kettle is much quicker and cheaper than boiling the spaghetti water on, in our case, a gas stove. The bottles always run out when you have not got

a) Any money.

b) And if you have, everywhere is closed for the night.

Annoying!!

Cook the spaghetti al dente, because you're going to add it to the frying pan.

Intersperse the spaghetti, cook for five minutes, add the feta. Turn off the hob. Add the grated Parmesan, add basil.

I'm hungry now!

Ingredients

One onion/shallots

Loads of garlic

Birdseye chilli x 2

One leek

A handful of mushrooms

Half a red pepper, half green pepper, half an orange pepper/ yellow pepper

A large handful of almonds with skin

Feta cheese

Parmesan to grate

Olive oil

Dark soy sauce

Wholewheat spaghetti

Basil leaves

Eggs and tomato

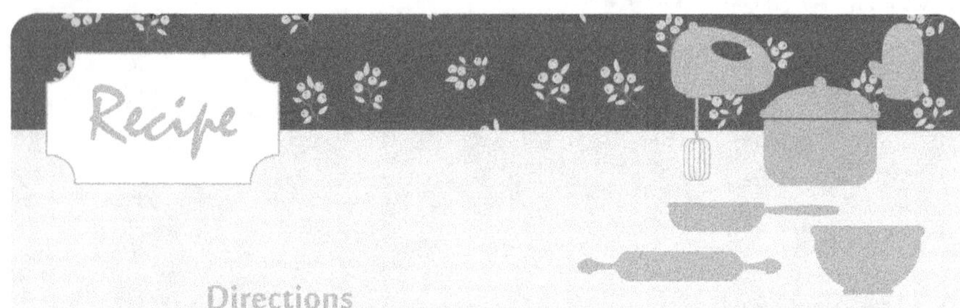

Directions

This recipe is very simple and delicious.
For two people.

Bread like ciabatta, sourdough, either warmed up in the oven (I put a bit of water around the outside) or toasted.

Take the garlic, squash it and then chop it quite large. Take a frying pan, heat up a good amount of olive oil, then add the garlic. Don't use too high a heat.

Add the cherry tomatoes, whole is fine, put the stove onto simmer, and leave it to cook for about twenty minutes, turning occasionaly. A lovely sauce will appear all around the tomatoes.

Add the eggs to tomato. Leave it cooking until the eggs look done.

Turn the heat off. Add the grated Parmesan, and basil. Salt & pepper to taste. We like a big dollop of harissa with ours. Dip the bread in the juice. Lovely.

Ingredients

Two 325g packs of cherry tomatoes, or equivalent

Four free range eggs

Parmesan to grate

Basil

A lot of garlic

Olive oil

Harrisa - Optional

Omelette with potato filling

Directions

This is great for any mash potato you have left over. In our case, very, very rare!

Heat some olive oil in a pan when hot add the garlic, onion, and the leek, in that order. Fry until brow. Add the peppers. Fry. Add the soy. Fry. Add the mash potato. Fold it, fold it until it's nice and brown then take it out, put it in a bowl.

Using the same pan, add a knob of butter to the oil. When it's really hot, add the eggs, salt and pepper, paprika, make an omelette. As soon as its starting to cook, add the mash potato filling to the top of omelette. Cook until the the omelette is brown. Then curl the two sides of omelette around the filling. In our case, the filling is so big it doesn't go anywhere near around it.

Serve with harissa.

Ingredients

Four free range eggs, whisked

Knob of butter

Olive oil

Paprika (optional)

For the stuffing:

Mash potato

Red or any colour peppers

Chilli

Leek

Parsnip

Onion/shallot

Loads of garlic

Harissa

Dark soy

Pepper

Salad a la caravan

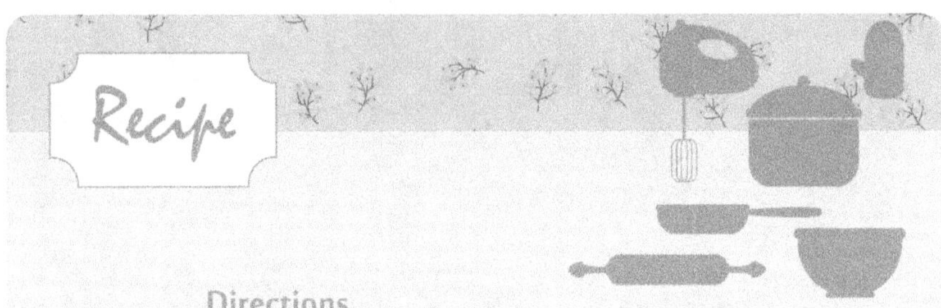

Directions

Chop, chop, chop all the ingredients, quarter the eggs, drain the tuna, and lay on a nice large bowl/plate.

Dressing from the maestro.

Olive oil - 3 tablespoons

Red wine vinegar - 1 tablespoon

Dijon mustard - tablespoon

Pepper

Salt

Finely chopped garlic

Whisk with a fork. Add to salad.

Ingredients

Cherry tomatoes

Little Gem Lettuce

Shallot x 2

Cucumber

Avocado

Celery

Eggs x 3

Tuna in spring water

Black olives

Humous

Harrissa - optional

Chickpea soup

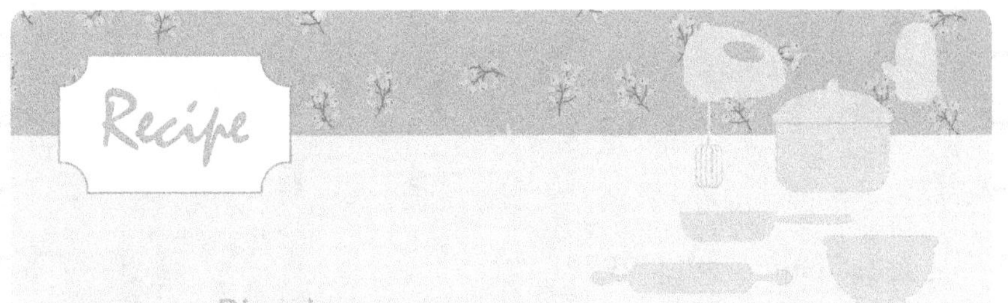

Directions

Drain, reserving the liquid, 2 cupfuls of chickpeas. Liquidise them using the chickpea water.

Heat the oil, add the celery and herbs. A second later the garlic. As soon as the garlic starts to brown, add the chopped tomatoes and cook together for a few minutes. Add the remaining chickpeas and coat them in the sauce for 5 minutes. If you've got some more of the chick pea water, add this, as you'll need about 250ml. If not, add water and you can also add a chicken/vegetable stock. Cover and simmer for 20 mins.

Add the lemon juice. Add more water if necessary.

Make some toast. While still hot rub it with the garlic, and chop up garlic to go on the top of toast. That'll keep you safe from Dracula!

Place a slice of bread in each soup bowl and pour the soup on top. Garnish with more sage leaves.

To serve:

4 small slices of bread

3 garlic cloves, peeled, crushed, then sliced in half, lengthways

Ingredients

225g of chickpeas. I usually use tinned.

3 tablespoons of olive oil

A celery stalk with leaves, finely chopped

Fresh sprig of rosemary, finely chopped

7 fresh sage leaves, finely chopped

More whole leaves for garnish (optional)

6 garlic cloves, peeled and crushed

1 small tin of chopped tomatoes

Juice of 1/2 lemon

Salt and pepper

Red chilli (optional)

Chicken/vegetable stock (optional)

Sourdough Bread

Lentil soup

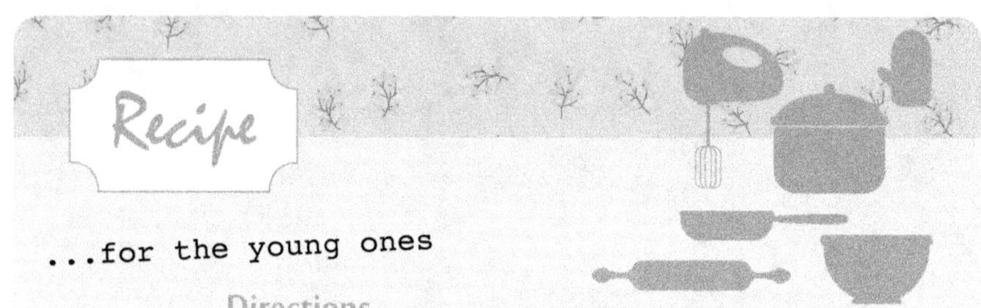

...for the young ones

Directions

Start cooking the onion, celery, carrot, parsnip, garlic in a saucepan using the olive oil. When they're brown and aromatic, add about 1 1/2 pints of water. When hot, add the chicken/ veg stock and the hot curry powder. Add the lentils. Simmer for about 25 min, stirring occasionally. Add some coriander to the top of each soup bowl. Eat with nan bread/ roti

Ingredients

1 onion

1 celery

1 carrot

1 parsnip

6 cloves of garlic

Hot curry powder

Lentils, rinse

Chicken/veg stock

Coriander

Two tablespoons of olive oil

Nan bread/ roti

Courgettes + Tomato with Halloumi

Directions

I love this!

Take a whole load of garlic - chopped quite big.

Slice the five courgettes.

Put olive oil in the frying pan, not too hot

Add the garlic.

Add the courgettes after five minutes.

Stir every so often until the courgettes are brown and shrunk.

Add the cherry tomatoes and do until the skin breaks.

Put in the oven which has heated up.

Add the sliced halloumi and when it's brown - it's done.

Make some toast, I personally like sourdough.

Put the courgette and tomato on the toast dribbling the olive oil.

Add Harissa.

Enjoy with Halloumi

Ingredients

Four courgettes
Eight cherry tomatoes
Loads of garlic
Olive oil
Halloumi
Sourdough bread

The Making of the Book

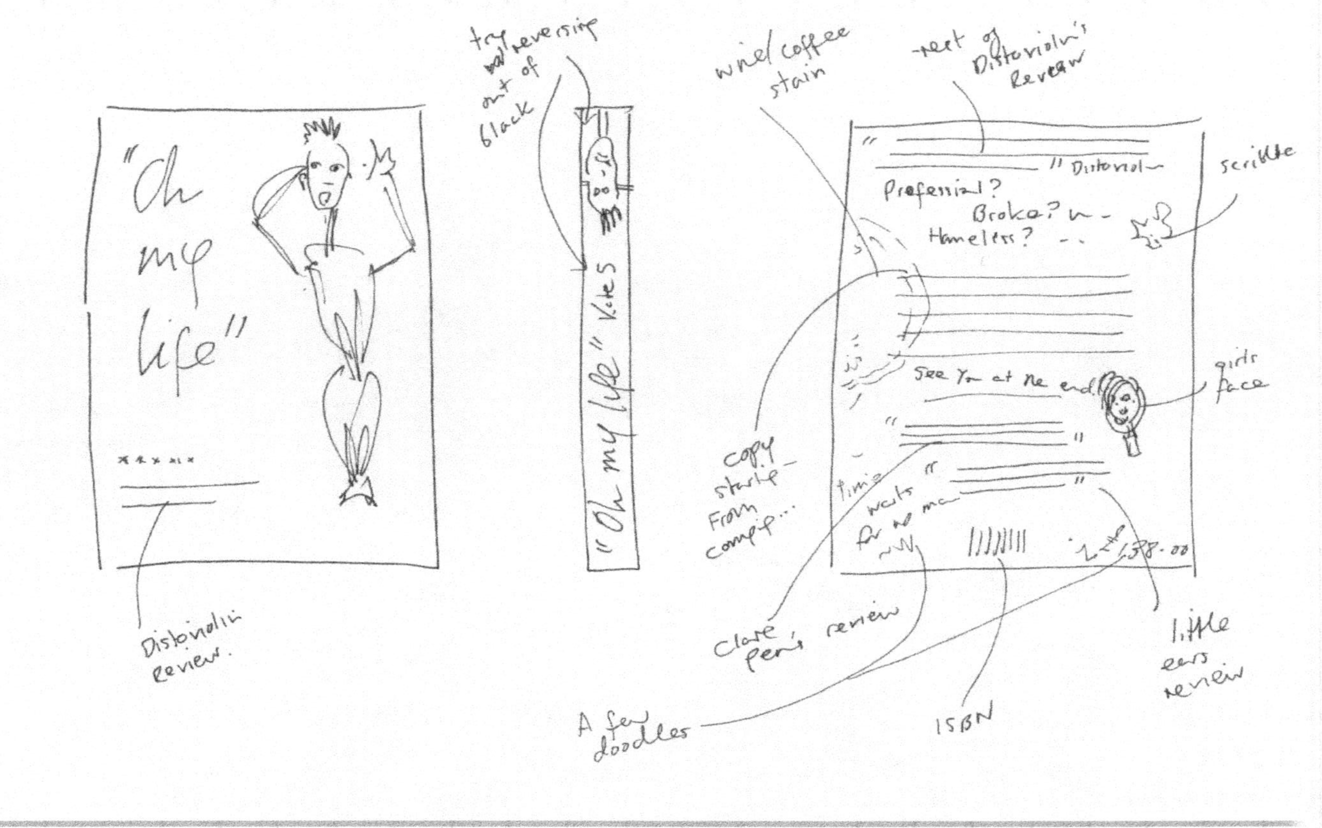

"Oh
my
life"
Distorviol review.
try reversing out of black
"Oh my life" Kites
wnel coffee stain
text of Distorviol's Review
scribble
"
" Distorviol
Professial?
Broka? w -
Homeless? -
See Yr at the end
girls face
copy strip from comp...
time waits for no man
Clare Peri's review
A few doodles
ISBN
little ears review

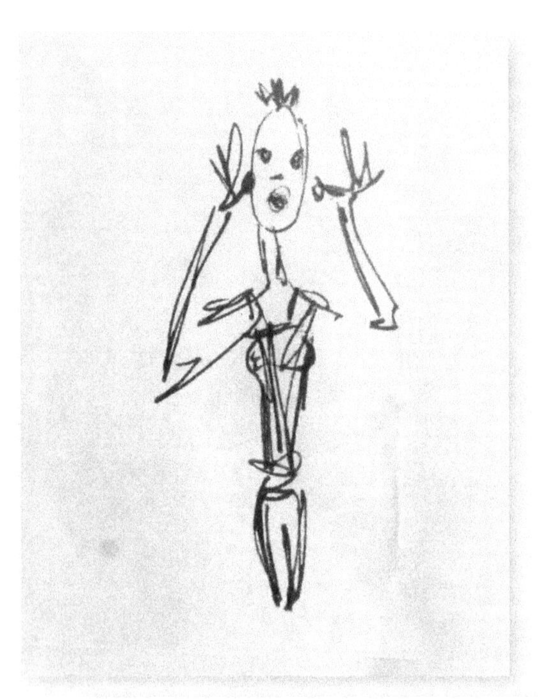

I'll
show
them!!

NEWS
BATHROOM YOU'D DIE FOR.....
help!
help!
help!

Party!
NEW
HEY!
HALLO!
Hipster!

I'll show them....

condom
this one

SUPER CAR!!!

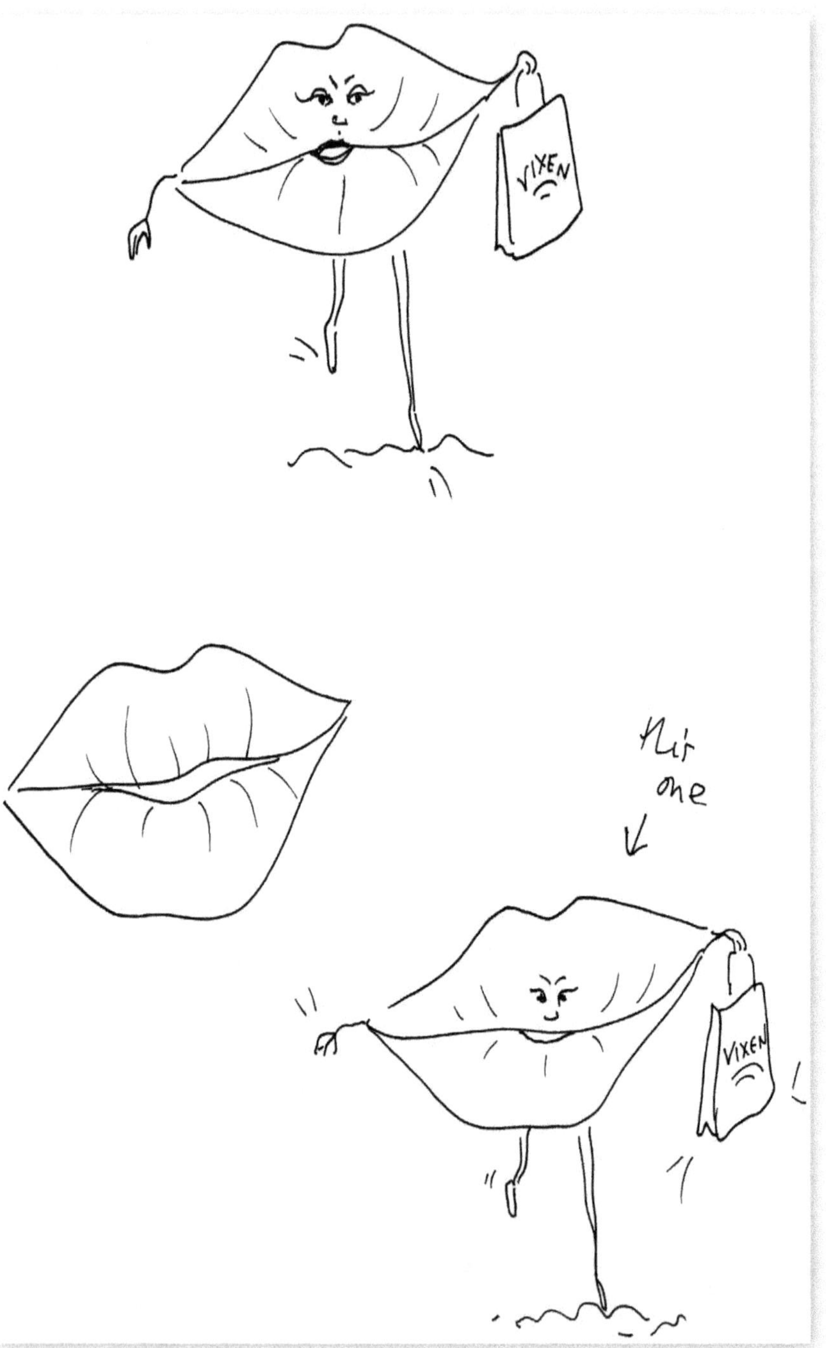

VIXEN
this
one
VIXEN

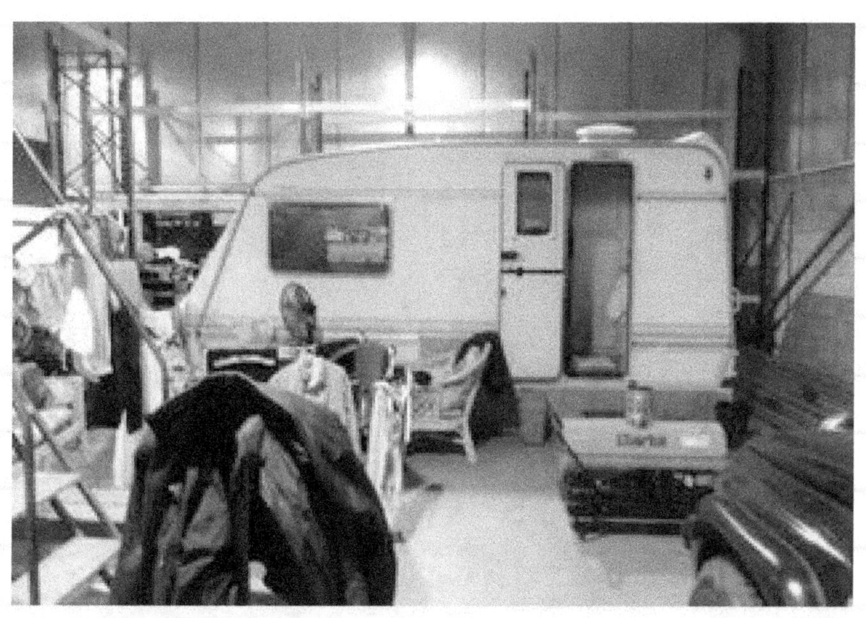

Me in Auckland

Alex in Milford Sounds

Clarke

"If you are going
through hell,
keep going"

— Winston Churchill

Dedication

For my father - without him I wouldn't have written this book.

Also to my mother, Tapio and my dear friend Laura.

A special thanks goes to Steph for all her patience and ability to decipher my notes and drawings, bringing them all to life.

And most of all to my very own little ears for everything. I'm so glad I met you.

Oh my Life

An extract
from my next book
about the care industry

WHO CARES?

You meet lots of care users in my job like the tea-cup urinator, what amazing precision! Stuffing knickers down anything that looks like a decorative bag. The manic walker/talker on sticks who races up and down the corridor apologising for everything.

I'm a domiciliary care/support worker for the elderly/ disabled who live in their own homes.

Let's talk about me first. I'm quite old by a carer's standards and have been one for a year. I did my induction course which was supposed to be three long days. The first day was cancelled and we whizzed through the course in two relatively short days.

I came out two days older but none the wiser.

I shadowed a few carers for the first two weeks, my first impressions of this new career were varying degrees of panic.

All carers had to have a car. That's because you have to drive around to people's houses using your petrol with only a very small petrol allowance from your company, plus all the other costs like MOT, insurance, tax, parking fines etc. are all yours.

The other thing you never have is time. You don't have any time between calls (carer's lingo) or if you do, it's five minutes. Not enough to go fifteen miles in heavy traffic. That's the reason why we all drive so fast. But if you do get a speeding ticket, guess who pays? It wouldn't be so bad if you earned loads-a-dosh, but you don't. Care worker's get the minimum wage.

So why do it?

It's a necessity first and foremost and beats being on

the dole. And some of the care users or clients are great, in fact I might rephrase that and say most of the clients.

No two hours are the same, I've seen as many as twenty people on some days, so you do have to think on your feet. Some situations you land up in are so funny, some are bizarre but others are incredibly distressing.

When I first started, lets just say I was green, even putrid green thinking of some of the items you have to dispose of. It's fairly stressful going to a user for the first time and you're hunting for the book where all the care workers write their notes.
Clients put their books is some bizarre places, like in a pillow, under sheets or they can't remember.

You invariably knock down items in your search, you try to correct it by knocking down something much bigger and feel very much like Inspector Clouseau. Meanwhile, the person is looking at you with either horror or anger. And, if you still can't find the book, you have to ask the user what the other care workers do ie. the ones that can find the****** book?

I remember this nice woman telling me what the other carers did which was to take off her pop socks and massage her very large legs with oil.

In fact, I should have made her lunch!

Old people are either very tiny or very big. Not too much in the middle. I was caring for a tiny one, and feeling under time pressure flew around the bed sitting room, pulling the duvet back to make the bed look inviting, making her a cup of tea in the tiny woman's tiny kitchen and after tripping over the bin, dropping a few things on the floor, just basic clumsiness, I rushed over to the window and pulled the blinds across with a flourish, knocking over one of her large and awful cacti, and breaking her pot as the earth exploded everywhere! The tiny woman held a tiny hand across her mouth and I felt awful as I said 'I'm so sorry...' I tried to clear it up, but a lot of it had gone behind the radiator. I wrote the truth in the carer's book and disappeared, tail between legs thinking, 'Whose caring for who…?'

Let me tell you about the attendance book and the care plan. And time. Most calls are half an hour. In that time you are supposed to read the care plan, quite a lengthy document about the care you should offer that individual person in their home, written by the care manager who works in the office. Then you have to fill out the attendance sheet with what you have offered to do on that visit. What I usually do is read the care workers attendance sheets which are dated and timed and suggest things that the user likes to have done which you repeat: I offered to take her to the toilet, and she accepted/refused or I offered to make her a cup of tea, sandwich, shower etc. which she declined/ accepted. This keeps you up to date and you can voice any concerns, which is important for the carer after you to know. And, gives you something to write on every visit.

You are rarely briefed on a new client, which can sometimes be extremely awkward. But, on this particular user, we were warned about him in UNDERLINED CAPS. 'WE WERE TO WAIT FOR THE OTHER CARER BEFORE ENTERING! NEVER GO IN ALONE. HE COLLECTS GUNS, THE POLICE KNOW ABOUT HIM AND WOULD GO IN FREQUENTLY ON GUN RAIDS. HE WORKED FOR THE SAS, (oh shit!) HE WAS NOW A PARAPLEGIC, WHO HAS A PERSONALITY DISORDER. NEVER INDULGE HIM WITH INFO ABOUT ANYTHING….' I was terrified before I even met him.

My new rota came out on Friday, I would scan down the list just in case I had him. He wasn't on my rota for the first three weeks. But then, HE WAS.

My first visit was bizarre and scary. I met the other carer, Michelle, outside. She was fat, ugly and smelt of BO. But she was a good carer and I got along with her quite well. She seemed to enjoy being ugly and smelling of BO and, come to think of it, fags.

Mr M had a video entry phone, quite apart from the cameras checking us out, and a complicated arrangement of locks to get through. On opening, we were met with Queen, FULL volume. I like LOAD MUSIC, and QUEEN but this was DEAFENINGLY LOUD. The house was completely kitted out for a paraplegic. He had an enormous flat-screened TV, a speedy electric wheelchair, gadgets galore, a hoist that ran off the ceiling and had rails in every room. Michelle danced in, wiggling her hips and shaking her arse to the music. She reminded me of that Disney character, Baloo. Mr M looked young and was good looking in a cold Arian way, his upper body was extremely fit. When he smiled, he was missing his top four teeth, I suspect that he had removed them. He was a bit Silence of the Lambs-ish and introduced himself, looking at me with his ice blue eyes.

I was terrified of him and felt like that cliche a rabbit in the headlights. Michelle was ok with him and had gone there quite a few times. She very efficiently helped him into his hoist, put on his neck brace and they made their way into his bedroom, he was in his electric hoist spinning across the ceiling, her dancing away on foot. She lowered him down, took off the hoist, and got him into bed. Then he looked at me and asked in a very pronounced way, 'Can you shave me?'

I haven't shaved anyone, only my legs in the bath. The idea of shaving him, talking to him, and hearing his stories about killing people in the SAS etc. Michelle said she would do it, so I had all his instructions to get a whole load of things to go around his bed that night. QUEEN WERE STILL ON FULL. Michelle was loudly singing to Bohemian Rhapsody, shaking her hips, and shaving him while I was killing time in the kitchen, trying to remember what I was getting. I don't know what it is about being nervous, I nod, but nothing really goes in. I had to fill up his cup to a certain level with coke, put the straw in a certain way, put the cup in a certain way on his table, but couldn't find the coke, or the special cups with a lids on, and all sorts of other things that had to be dotted around his bed, in a certain way. I kept getting things wrong, couldn't see things that were right in front of me etc. We were in there for an hour instead of half an hour, which wasn't entirely my fault. I was so relieved just to get out of there alive.

Locks, key codes and I, are not necessarily well suited, although I do try. Virtually all care users have a key code box which is small, black and mounted on the wall by the front door. All care workers have a file, with name of the care user and their different four number codes. Pressing these digits allows the box to be opened and from inside you get the front door keys. But, if stressed, you can search for someone's name and number on the list, but you can't actually see it although in most cases it's there. It would help if the names were alphabetical, but they're not. If you do find the code and accomplish getting the keys out of the black box, you either have to wrestle with the front door lock or you are unable to get the keys out. Or, sometimes it doesn't open at all. On some key codes, you have to line the four numbers up in a row like you do on a padlock, and the numbers are very small. I wear a contact lens for driving, so have be a long way back to check that all the numbers are lined up. Sometimes it's dark, so you have to use a torch if you have one. Sometimes, you don't get as far as the above. Or, if you do get the black box open, the keys just drop out and you are left scrabbling about on the ground, in the dark, trying to find the keys in various flower pots, drains etc. thinking what the hell am I doing this for. I swear, my hair's gone a lot greyer since I started as a care worker. In the meantime, inside, the care user is listening to loads of cursing, scuffling, keys or torch being dropped on ground, more cursing etc.

It's important to be cheerful when you do get in, providing the care user doesn't knock you out thinking that you're a burglar.

In most cases, you are the users main link to life outside and I was certainly this woman in Wylie's link.

I went in, without the usual difficulty and cheerfully called out:

"hello??"

"hello??"

As I was opening various doors and peering inside.

I went into a dark room, nothing in there except a fairly disgusting 'used commode'. But then, I spun around when I heard her whispering 'hello deeaar' from right behind my head. She was tiny, in a wheelchair with a deathly white face, long, thin greasy brown hair and was missing a leg. She didn't stay still, she kept darting around me, looking me up and down from all angles very like a Hans Christian Anderson's witch. She peered forward, eyes almost out on sticks, saying 'is that right deeaar' 'oh yes deeaar', 'yes…oh yes' head on one side. I expected her to push a bony finger against my ribs to check I was plump enough for eating.

She also looked like she had an erection under her skirt, but it was just her sawn off thighbone sticking up. Luckily, she only wanted a cup of tea, to show me all her millions of pills she was on daily, and her family photographs. She also dropped in that she would probably lose her second leg quite soon. I exited there quite sharply.

Outside, Alex was waiting for me I had just moved in with him the weekend before starting work. He had a job in Salisbury starting 8am-5.30pm. I would meet him after if I was doing an evening shift, and he would drive me in his van. I/we had to work every other weekend. He couldn't have been greater. He would help me with the door codes, find the keys when I dropped them, always had a torch, and when the doors were stiff he would open them, then crouch down so he wasn't seen as I said 'hello...hello..'

Sometimes, it was a close call. On one occasion, I couldn't use the microwave and it was a relatively new client. She was 100 years old, and had not been downstairs for twenty-five years! I thought it would be safe for Alex to come in, he quickly showed me how to use it but as we turned around, she was standing in the doorway, smiling.

She had a neighbour who used to keep her supplied with chocolate and biscuits and was living like a tramp, but seemed happy enough. Her neighbour was not that capable any more, he was old and had mental health issues, so my Care Company got funding to visit her.

When I first went there, I was a bit shocked. It was one of the many incidents that you are not briefed on. I couldn't find anyone at all downstairs, so I crept upstairs. It really smelt up there, and there were flies everywhere. I went into various rooms, knocking on doors, and then found her sitting in a chair smiling. Her hair was matted, her legs and ankles were streaked with dark brown (!) she was wearing a brown holey sweater, and a brown holey skirt, no pants and her finger and toenails were so long they had curled round and round and round and round. She had various teacups dotted around, which on closer inspection, contained urine. Rotten bananas, rubbish, curdled milk, upset coffee, a kettle, but no tv, no books, no radio, only her own thoughts.

I phoned up my office and explained that she didn't have any food or any milk and was urinating in tea-cups. We got hold of a social worker, and they were able to get her some food, started up a delivery of milk, and a few more visits from us.

I liked her, she was artistic and had lots of drawings. She had made various ornaments like cats, dogs and pigs out of clay. At least i think it was clay!

She showed me her treasures which had sentimental value to her, as treasures should. She started coming downstairs a bit more. She had a nice kitchen and lounge that was stuck in the 70's and hadn't been used since then, all very neat compared to upstairs. I suggested that she should live down here. She had a big armchair, which looked a lot more comfortable than her chair upstairs. She very carefully sat down in it. I went into the kitchen to prepare her lunch. When I went back, she was struggling, her face all red, trying to get up! I helped her but it was quite a struggle. She went back upstairs again and that was that.

I used to see her twice a day, heat her food (thanks Alex!) in the microwave, make her tea or coffee, ham sandwiches, cheese, fruit. But, the last time I saw her, she had done a shit on a piece of paper on the living room floor. She seemed to find this very amusing, I could never stop her urinating in teacups and was very grateful for my apron and gloves. But, to my shame, I left it for the next carer.

Glove talk….

One of my first visits was to a bed bound woman, back strainingly huge. I don't really know what was wrong with her, maybe if I had more time to read the care plan I would ;)

On every user you have to wear surgical gloves, but in this case it was recommended that you 'double glove'. There's nothing worse than your nail piercing through your glove, while you're 'cleaning' her, or anyone else's nether regions. Short nails are another must. You also have to wear a plastic apron, which you dispose of after each user.

If someone is bed bound you have to work in two's. It's actually quite amazing how seamless washing, dressing, putting on a new pad was AFTER A WHILE. We rolled her from one to the other to wash her, we lifted her on the count of three, one, two, three to put on a bra, dress and cardigan, you put on everything over the head. We would roll this particular person onto her bedpan, she would do rip roaring farts and the rest, we'd just raise our eyes to the ceiling, trying not to snigger. We saw her four times a day, and used to take it in turns to clean her. Not a pleasant task.

Must have gone through a pack a day of jumbo size baby wipes. I'm not big, but a lot of people couldn't hold her so I preferred to be on the 'holding side', quite often she would fart loudly in the face of various carers. We all hated doing her, and she would lie with her eyes closed throughout. Meanwhile, her husband used to sit and watch TV. He was luckily deaf. She had a very close and huge family who were always about, could be six people in the lounge where she lay in her hospital bed, in full view of the TV.

Luckily, we lost her to another care company, which was great for us carers.